WHAT'S COOKING
Mexican

Marlena Spieler

This is a Parragon Book
First published in 2000

Parragon
Queen Street House
4 Queen Street
Bath BA1 1HE, UK

ISBN: 0-75254-042-4

Printed in Singapore

ACKNOWLEDGEMENTS

Editorial Consultant: Felicity Jackson
Photography: Colin Bowling, Paul Forrester and Stephen Brayne
Home Economist and Stylist: Vicki Smallwood

All props supplied by Barbara Stewart at Surfaces.

NOTE

Cup measurements in this book are for American cups.
All-purpose flour is measured in scooped cups. Tablespoons are
assumed to be 15ml. Unless otherwise stated, milk is assumed to be full fat,
eggs are medium and pepper is freshly ground black pepper.

Recipes using uncooked eggs should be
avoided by infants, the elderly, pregnant women and anyone
suffering from an illness.

Contents

Introduction

The cuisine of Mexico is a diverse and extraordinary cuisine, a complex layering of cultures, starting with the ancient Indian civilizations and built upon by the Spanish conquest as well as other European rulers and influences.

The soul of Mexican food lies in its ancient roots: Aztec, Toltec, Zapotec, Ohnec and Mayan. Deeply coloured, complex, rich sauces made of mild and hot chillies, seeds, herbs and vegetables are as ancient as the cultures from which they come. Long-stewed meats, such as the Spanish contribution of pork, figure prominently in the Mexican kitchen; the broth that comes about through the cooking makes soups that fuel everyday life and add flavour and depth to dishes of beans, rice and stews. Fish from the coastlines that cover thousands of miles and define the shape of the country, are eaten cloaked with spicy pastes, splashed with chillies, wrapped in tortillas or fragrant leaves.

Over this ancient cuisine of indigenous foods and techniques lies a veneer of Spanish propriety and European tradition, as well as the imports from Spain: wheat (for those flour tortillas and the crusty bread rolls, bolillos), domesticated animals whose milk added cheese to the menu, and the pig! With the abundant fat provided by the pig, frying became possible, adding a new dimension to the cooking methods.

TORTILLAS

The tortilla – a thin pancake-like flat bread – is eaten for nearly every meal throughout Mexico. Served in the same way as bread to accompany dishes, they are also wrapped around food as an eating utensil.

In the north, wheat or flour tortillas will be the ones you will find most often; in the south they will be corn, sometimes blue corn. Tortilla may be tiny or huge, eaten fresh off the griddle (*comal*) or filled and fried; they form the basis of the foods of Mexico.

Wrapped around any filling, a corn tortilla becomes a taco, a flour tortilla a burrito. Fresh and warm, a corn tortilla is a soft taco, fried to a crisp it is a crisp taco. A flat crisply fried tortilla is a tostada – top them with a layer of warm refried beans, cheese, pickled chillies or salsa, salad and morsels of meat or vegetables.

Stale corn tortillas are never thrown away in the frugal Mexican kitchen, and the cuisine is all the better for it: dipped into spicy sauces then rolled around various fillings they make the wonderful casserole that is called enchiladas, or fried and layered with sauce they are called chilaquiles.

Most of us are familiar with tortilla chips – at their best when freshly made from stale corn tortillas, but also widely available in packets.

BEANS

Beans, too, are basic, with rice and chillies. In every marketplace café (*fonda*) and home kitchen, you'll find pots and *cazuelas* of simmering beans, ready to be eaten in all of their guises, or just from a bowl with a few tortillas to roll around them to satisfy hunger.

Throughout Mexico, the types of beans vary delightfully, from the tender pale pink beans of the north, such as pinto, to the inky black beans of the south. Beans that are puréed and cooked in fat and spices are called refried beans, though they are not really fried at all, merely cooked down to an intense paste in a puddle of (traditional) lard or (contemporary) vegetable oil.

CHILLIES

Next to tortillas and beans, it is chillies that define Mexican food. They offer flavour, textures, colours and aromas as well as heat, and keep the often monotonous diet lively. They are eaten raw and cooked, sliced and stewed, stuffed and puréed, soaked and fried, and are eaten at every meal, usually in the form of a salsa to spoon on as desired. They are rich in anti-oxidant vitamins and will clear your sinuses pronto, not to mention their alleged aphrodisiac qualities.

Understandably, chillies can intimidate – they can be searingly hot, and should be added a little at a time.

Mild chillies are usually eaten red and dried, though Mexicans also dote on crushed hot red chillies – usually a dried cayenne. Mild chillies, such as pasilla, ancho, mulatto and negro, make up the distinctive flavourful mixture sold simply on our spice shelf as 'mild chilli powder'.

Most fresh chillies are hot and hotter. Jalapeño are probably most often eaten, a good all purpose little chilli with a nice fiery heat and delicious flavour. Serrano is another popular fresh chilli. In the Caribbean region habanero and Scotch bonnet peppers add their distinctive fire.

Two milder chillies, the anaheim and poblano are utterly delicious eaten stuffed, as you would a pepper; if unavailable, use ordinary green peppers, roasted and marinated with a chopped fresh hot chilli or two to enliven them.

Bottled hot seasonings are ubiquitous, too; you'll find one on practically every table as well as kitchen shelf: a nice jolt of tangy fire for those who dare.

OTHER FLAVOURINGS

Mexican spicing, however, is not limited to chillies: cinnamon, cloves, black pepper, cocoa powder and especially cumin are used with enthusiasm, as are the herbs of oregano, marjoram, mint, epazote and fresh coriander (cilantro). Roasted onion and whole garlic cloves are often crushed to form the basis of a sauce, and wedges of lime or lemon are served with soups, meats, fish, almost everything, Mediterranean–style.

MEXICAN STYLE

Meals in Mexico are a never ending fiesta. The main meal, the *comida corrida*, is served Spanish style, in the afternoon. Breakfast may either be a light one of hot chocolate or coffee with sweet rolls or *churros* to dip in, or a hearty late breakfast *almuerzo*, often consisting of the exquisite egg dishes which Mexico is well known for. The markets and their *fondas*, *cantinas* and *taquerias*, beckon with their irresistible aromas, convincing you that you are indeed hungry, and an endless parade of tacos, tostadas, enchiladas, burritos, soups, shellfish, grilled fish tantalise the palate.

And if your appetite is jaded from the sultry heat and feasting, and you don't have room for even one more burrito, persuade yourself to nibble a reviving snack – fresh fruit, such as pineapple, oranges and mango – sprinkled with hot red pepper and served with a squeeze of lime juice. After that you will be ready for anything.

Soups & Starters

Start your meal in authentic Mexican style with a bowl of homemade soup. Mexican soups are distinctive and varied, ranging from light soups of plain stock served with a spoonful of salsa and a little lime, to hearty one-bowl meals such as Pozole. Whatever your soup, expect to find it served with a wedge of lime, lemon or orange, a sprinkling of pungent fresh coriander and a hint of hot chilli.

Little niblles, to, are an important part of any Mexican meal. The world-famous Guacamole, mashed avocado with seasonings and spices, makes the most perfect appetizer I know – delicious with crunchy tortilla chips and a killing Mexican beer or a shot of Tequila. Spicy-sweet Meat Empanadas, filled with savoury meat, aromatic spices and nuts, are as moreish as they are unusual, and you can keep them in your freezer ready to take out for an impromptu party, anytime.

With its thousands of miles of coastline, seafood cocktails and marinated fish make cooling, refreshing and utterly light appetizers, to start a Mexican feast. Alternatively, you could serve tiny tacos, rolls of tortillas filled with tantalising Mexican mixtures, or a salad of crunchy raw vegetables spiced with chillies. Whatever your taste, you will surely be enticed by the recipes in this chapter.

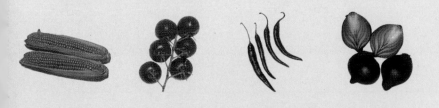

Yucatecan Citrus Soup

Roasted onion and garlic are combined with tangy citrus flavours to create a soup full of tantalising tastes.

Serves 4

INGREDIENTS

2 onions
15 large garlic cloves, unpeeled
1 tbsp extra-virgin olive oil
1.3 litres/2¼ pints/6 cups vegetable,
 chicken or fish stock
225 ml/8 fl oz/1 cup water
8 ripe tomatoes, diced
pinch of dried oregano

1 fresh green chilli, such as jalapeño
 or serrano, deseeded and chopped
pinch of ground cumin
½ tsp finely grated grapefruit rind
½ tsp finely grated lime rind
½ tsp finely grated orange rind
juice and diced flesh of 2 limes
juice of 1 orange

juice of 1 grapefruit
salt and pepper

TO GARNISH:
tortilla chips, or sliced tortilla strips
 fried until crisp
2 tbsp chopped fresh coriander
 (cilantro)

1 Half one unpeeled onion. Peel and finely chop the other.

2 Heat a large heavy-based frying pan (skillet), add the unpeeled onion halves and garlic and cook over a medium-high heat until the skins char and the onions are caramelized on their cut sides; the garlic should be soft on the inside. Remove from the pan and allow to cool slightly.

3 Meanwhile, heat the oil in a pan and lightly sauté the remaining onion until softened. Add the stock and water and bring to the boil. Reduce the heat and simmer for a few minutes.

4 Peel the charred onion and garlic, then chop coarsely and add to the simmering soup, together with the tomatoes, oregano, chilli and cumin. Cook

for about 15 minutes, stirring the soup occasionally.

5 Add the citrus rind, season with salt and pepper, then simmer for a further 2 minutes. Remove from the heat and stir in the lime flesh and citrus juices.

6 Ladle into soup bowls, garnish with tortilla chips and fresh coriander (cilantro) and serve .

Spicy Gazpacho

This classic Spanish cold soup is given a Mexican twist by adding chillies and fresh coriander (cilantro). Serve with chunks of bread for a refreshing start to a meal.

Serves 4–6

INGREDIENTS

1 cucumber
2 green (bell) peppers
6 ripe flavourful tomatoes
½ fresh hot chilli
½–1 onion, finely chopped
3–4 garlic cloves, chopped
4 tbsp extra-virgin olive oil

¼ –½ tsp ground cumin
2–4 tsp sherry vinegar, or a
  combination of balsamic vinegar
  and wine vinegar
4 tbsp chopped fresh coriander
  (cilantro)
2 tbsp chopped fresh parsley

300 ml/10 fl oz/1¼ cups vegetable or
  chicken stock
600 ml/1 pint/2½ cups tomato juice
  or canned crushed tomatoes
salt and pepper
ice cubes, to serve

1 Cut the cucumber in half lengthways, cut into quarters. Remove the seeds with a teaspoon, then dice the flesh. Cut the (bell) peppers in half, remove the cores and seeds, then dice the flesh.

2 If you prefer to skin the tomatoes, place in a heatproof bowl, pour boiling water over to cover and stand for 30 seconds. Drain and plunge into cold water. The skins will then slide off easily. Cut the tomatoes in half, deseed if

wished, then chop the flesh. Deseed and chop the chilli.

3 Combine half the cucumber, green (bell) pepper, tomatoes and onion in a blender or food processor with all the chilli, garlic, olive oil, cumin, vinegar, coriander (cilantro) and parsley. Process with enough stock for a smooth purée.

4 Pour the puréed soup into a bowl and stir in the remaining stock and tomato juice. Add the

remaining green (bell) pepper, cucumber, tomatoes and onion, stirring well. Season with salt and pepper to taste, then cover and chill for a few hours.

5 Ladle into bowls and serve with ice cubes in each bowl.

VARIATION

Freeze tomato juice ice cubes as a delicious alternative.

Spicy Courgette (Zucchini) Soup with Rice & Lime

Mild red chilli powder and pan-browned garlic give flavour to this simple, homely soup. Quick to make, it's ideal for a light lunch.

Serves 4

INGREDIENTS

2 tbsp oil
4 garlic cloves, thinly sliced
1–2 tbsp mild red chilli powder
¼–½ tsp ground cumin

1.5 litres/2¾ pints/6¼ cups chicken, vegetable or beef stock
2 courgettes (zucchini), cut into bite-sized chunks

4 tbsp long-grain rice
salt and pepper
fresh oregano sprigs, to garnish
lime wedges, to serve (optional)

1 Heat the oil in a heavy-based pan, add the garlic and fry for about 2 minutes until softened and just beginning to change colour. Add the chilli powder and cumin and cook over a medium-low heat for a minute.

2 Stir in the stock, courgettes (zucchini) and rice, then cook over a medium-high heat for about 10 minutes until the courgettes (zucchini) are just tender and the rice is cooked through. Season the soup with salt and pepper.

3 Ladle into soup bowls, garnish with oregano and serve with lime wedges.

VARIATION

Instead of rice, use rice-shaped pasta, such as orzo or semone de melone, or very thin pasta known as fideo. Use yellow summer squash instead of the courgettes (zucchini) and add cooked pinto beans in place of the rice. Diced tomatoes also make a tasty addition.

COOK'S TIP

Choose courgettes (zucchini) which are firm to the touch and have shiny skin. They should not be too large.

Mexican Vegetable Soup
with Tortilla Chips

*Crisp tortilla chips act as croûtons in this hearty vegetable soup which is found throughout Mexico.
Add cheese to melt in, if you wish, and make the soup as hot tasting as you like!*

Serves 4–6

INGREDIENTS

2 tbsp vegetable or extra-virgin
  olive oil
1 onion, finely chopped
4 garlic cloves, finely chopped
¼–½ tsp ground cumin
2–3 tsp mild chilli powder, such as
  ancho or New Mexico
1 carrot, sliced
1 waxy potato, diced
350 g/12 oz/1½ cups diced fresh or
  canned tomatoes

1 courgette (zucchini),
  diced
¼ small cabbage, shredded
1 litre/1¾ pints/4 cups vegetable or
  chicken stock or water
1 corn-on-the-cob, the kernels cut
  off the cob, or canned sweetcorn
about 10 green or runner beans,
  topped and tailed, then cut into
  bite-sized lengths
salt and pepper

TO SERVE:
4–6 tbsp chopped fresh coriander
  (cilantro)
salsa of your choice, or chopped
  fresh chilli, to taste
tortilla chips

1 Heat the oil in a heavy-based pan. Add the onion and garlic and cook for a few minutes until softened, then sprinkle in the cumin and chilli powder. Stir in the carrot, potato, tomatoes, courgettes (zucchini) and cabbage and cook for 2 minutes, stirring the mixture occasionally.

2 Pour in the stock. Cover and cook over a medium heat for about 20 minutes until the vegetables are tender.

3 Add extra water if necessary, then stir in the sweetcorn and green beans and cook for a further 5–10 minutes or until the beans are tender. Season with salt and pepper to taste, bearing in mind that the tortilla chips may be salty.

4 Ladle the soup into soup bowls and sprinkle each portion with fresh coriander (cilantro). Top with a dab of salsa, then add a handful of tortilla chips.

Crab & Cabbage Soup

From the Vera Cruz region, this delicious soup uses fresh crab meat to add a rich flavour to a mildly spicy vegetable and fish broth.

Serves 4

INGREDIENTS

¼ cabbage
450 g/1 lb ripe tomatoes
1 litre/1¾ pints/4 cups fish stock
    or water mixed with 1–2 fish
    stock cubes
1 onion, thinly sliced
1 small carrot, diced

4 garlic cloves, finely chopped
6 tbsp chopped fresh coriander
    (cilantro)
1 tsp mild chilli powder, such as
    New Mexico
1 whole cooked crab or
    175–225 g/6–8 oz crab meat

1 tbsp torn fresh oregano leaves
salt and pepper

TO SERVE:
1–2 limes, cut into wedges
salsa of your choice

1 Cut out any thick stalk from the cabbage, then shred finely using a large knife.

2 To skin the tomatoes, place in a heatproof bowl, pour boiling water over to cover and stand for 30 seconds. Drain and plunge into cold water. The skins will then slide off easily. Next, chop the skinned tomatoes.

3 Place the tomatoes and stock in a pan with the onion, carrot, cabbage, garlic, fresh coriander (cilantro) and chilli powder. Bring to the boil, then reduce the heat and simmer for about 20 minutes until the vegetables are just tender.

4 Remove the crab meat from the whole crab, if using. Twist off the legs and claws and crack with a heavy knife. Remove the flesh from the legs with a skewer; leave the cracked claws intact, if wished. Remove the body section from the main crab shell and remove the meat, discarding the stomach bag and feathery gills.

5 Add the oregano and crab meat to the pan and simmer for 10–15 minutes to combine the flavours. Season the mixture with salt and pepper.

6 Ladle into deep soup bowls and serve with 1–2 wedges of lime. Hand round the salsa separately.

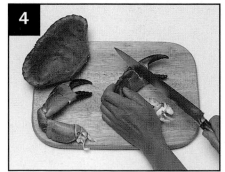

Mexican Fish
& Roasted Tomato Soup

Mexico's long shoreline yields an abundance of fish and shellfish, which are
often turned into spicy, satisfying soups.

Serves 4

INGREDIENTS

5 ripe tomatoes
5 garlic cloves, unpeeled
500 g/1 lb 2 oz snapper, cut into
  chunks

1 litre/1¾ pints/4 cups fish stock, or
  water plus a fish stock cube or two
2–3 tbsp olive oil
1 onion, chopped

2 fresh chillies, such as serrano,
  deseeded and thinly sliced
lime wedges, to serve

1 Heat an ungreased heavy-based frying pan (skillet), add the whole tomatoes and garlic and char over a high heat or under a preheated grill (broiler). The skins of the vegetables should blacken and char, and the flesh inside should be tender. Alternatively, place the tomatoes and garlic cloves in a roasting tin (pan) and bake in a preheated oven at 190–200°C/375–400°F/Gas Mark 5–6 for about 40 minutes.

2 Leave the tomatoes and garlic to cool, then remove the skins and chop coarsely, combining them with any juices from the pan. Set aside.

3 Poach the snapper in the stock over medium just until it is opaque and firmish. Remove from the heat and set aside.

4 Heat the oil in a pan and cook the chopped onion until softened. Strain in the cooking liquid from the fish, then add the coarsley chopped tomatoes and garlic, and stir.

5 Bring to the boil, then reduce the heat and simmer for about 5 minutes to combine the flavours. Add the serrano chillies.

6 Divide chunks of the poached fish between soup bowls, ladle over the hot soup and serve with lime wedges for squeezing over the top.

Chicken, Avocado & Chipotle Soup

This soup evolved from the foodstalls that line the streets of Tlalpan, a suburb of Mexico City: rich avocado, shreds of chicken and the smoky hit of chipotle make it special.

Serves 4

INGREDIENTS

1.5 litres/2¾ pints/6¼ cups chicken stock
2–3 garlic cloves, finely chopped
1–2 chipotle chillies, cut into very thin strips (see Cook's Tip)
1 avocado
lime or lemon juice, for tossing

3–5 spring onions (scallions), thinly sliced
350–400 g/12–14 oz cooked chicken breast meat, torn or cut into shreds or thin strips
2 tbsp chopped fresh coriander (cilantro)

TO SERVE:
1 lime, cut into wedges
handful of tortilla chips (optional)

1 Place the stock in a pan with the garlic and chipotle chillies and bring to the boil.

2 Meanwhile, cut the avocado in half around the stone (pit). Twist apart, then remove the stone (pit) with a knife. Carefully peel off the skin, dice the flesh and toss in lime or lemon juice to prevent discoloration.

3 Arrange the spring onions (scallions), chicken, avocado and fresh coriander (cilantro) in the base of 4 soup bowls or in a large serving bowl.

4 Ladle hot stock over, and serve with lime and a handful of tortilla chips if using.

VARIATION

Add a drained 400 g/14 oz can chick-peas (garbanzo beans) to the bowls in Step 3.

COOK'S TIP

Chipotle chillies are smoked and dried jalapeño chillies and are available canned or dried from specialist stores. They add a distinctive smoky flavour to dishes and are very hot. Use chipotles canned in adobo marinade for this recipe, if possible. Drain the canned version before using. Dried chipotles need to be reconstituted before using (see page 100).

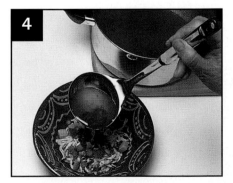

Big Pot of Simmered Meat

*The Mexican kitchen traditionally simmers big chunks of meat, which gives two meals in one:
tender boiled meat for tacos or enchiladas, as well as a hearty rich stock for soups and rice.*

Serves 6

INGREDIENTS

2 kg/4 lb 8 oz beef, pork, chicken
   for stewing – any combination or
   just one type
2 onions, chopped
1 whole garlic bulb, divided into
   cloves and peeled

several sprigs of fresh herbs, such
   as parsley, oregano, coriander
   (cilantro)
1 carrot, sliced
1–2 stock cubes
salt and pepper

cooked macaroni or thin noodles, to
   serve
finely sliced spring onions (scallions),
   to garnish

1 Place the meat in a large pan and cover with cold water. Bring to the boil and skim off the scum that forms on the surface. Reduce the heat and add the onions, garlic, herbs and carrot. Simmer, covered, for 1 hour.

2 Add the stock cubes and salt and pepper to taste. (If using a combination of meat and chicken, cook the meat first for 1 hour, then add the chicken.) Continue to simmer over a very low heat for about 2 hours until the meat is very tender.

3 Remove from the heat and allow the meat to cool in the stock. Using a slotted spoon, transfer the meat to a board and shred; set aside. Skim the fat from the stock, or leave to chill then remove the fat by simply lifting it off. Strain the soup for a clearer soup. Reheat before serving.

4 To serve, spoon the hot macaroni or noodles into soup bowls, then top with the shredded meat and ladle over the soup. Garnish with spring onions (scallions) and serve.

VARIATION

For a simple soup to make from the strained stock, cook diced courgettes (zucchini) in the stock with a cinnamon stick; remove and discard the cinnamon stick, then serve the soup with a wedge of lime, a dash of salsa to taste and a sprinkling of fresh coriander (cilantro).

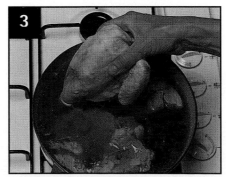

Beef & Vegetable Soup

A wonderful meal-in-a-bowl, this soup is ideal for a winter supper or lunch.
The beefy flavour, enhanced with spices, is very warming.

Serves 4–6

INGREDIENTS

225 g/8 oz tomatoes
2 corn-on-the-cobs
1 litre/1¾ pints/4 cups beef soup or
   stock, following the recipe on page
   22, or use a chilled ready-made
   stock
1 carrot, thinly sliced

1 onion, chopped
1–2 small waxy potatoes, diced
¼ cabbage, thinly sliced
¼ tsp ground cumin
¼ tsp mild chilli powder
¼ tsp paprika
225 g/8 oz cooked beef (preferably

from the recipe on page 22), cut
   into bite-sized pieces
3–4 tbsp chopped fresh coriander
   (cilantro) (optional)
hot salsa, such as Scorched Chilli
   Salsa (see page 102), to serve

1 To skin the tomatoes, place in a heatproof bowl, pour boiling water over to cover and stand for 30 seconds. Drain and plunge into cold water. The skins will then slide off easily. Chop the tomatoes.

2 Using a large knife, cut the corn-on-the-cobs into 2.5 cm/1 inch pieces.

3 Place the stock in a pan with the tomatoes, carrot, onion, potatoes and cabbage. Bring to the boil, then reduce the heat and simmer for 10–15 minutes or until the vegetables are tender.

4 Add the corn-on-the-cob pieces, the cumin, chilli powder, paprika and beef pieces. Bring back to the boil over a medium heat.

5 Ladle into soup bowls and serve sprinkled with fresh coriander (cilantro), if using, with salsa handed round separately.

COOK'S TIP

To thicken the soup and give it a flavour of the popular Mexican steamed dumplings, known as a tamale, add a few tablespoons of masa harina, mixed into a thinnish paste with a little water, at Step 4. Stir well, then continue cooking until thickened.

Pozole

The dish of hulled maize kernels – hominy – simmered in rich stock is eaten all over Mexico, and is served with lots of fresh garnishes: shredded cabbage, onion, fried tortilla or crisp fried pork skin (chicharrones), and of course, chillies and lime wedges.

Serves 4

INGREDIENTS

450 g/1 lb pork for stewing, such as
   lean belly
½ small chicken
about 2 litres/3½ pints/8 cups water
1 chicken stock cube
1 whole garlic bulb, divided into
   cloves but not peeled

1 onion, chopped
2 bay leaves
450 g/1 lb canned or cooked
   hominy or chick-peas
   (garbanzo beans)
¼–½ tsp ground cumin
salt and pepper

TO SERVE:
½ small cabbage, thinly shredded
fried pork skin
dried oregano leaves
dried chilli flakes
tortilla chips
lime wedges

1 Place the pork and chicken in a large pan. Add enough water to fill the pan. (Do not worry about having too much stock – it is wonderful for the rest of the week, and freezes well.)

2 Bring to the boil, then skim off the scum that rises to the surface. Reduce the heat and add the stock cube, garlic, onion and bay leaves. Simmer, covered, over a medium-low heat until the pork and chicken are both tender and cooked through.

3 Using a slotted spoon, remove the pork and chicken from the soup and leave to cool. When cool enough to handle, remove the chicken flesh from the bones and cut into small pieces. Then, cut the pork into bite-sized pieces. Set aside.

4 Skim the fat off the soup and discard the bay leaves. Add the hominy or chick-peas (garbanzo beans) and cumin, salt and pepper to taste. Bring to the boil.

5 To serve, place a little pork and chicken in soup bowls. Top with cabbage, fried pork skin, oregano and chilli flakes, then spoon in the hot soup. Serve with tortilla chips and lime as wished.

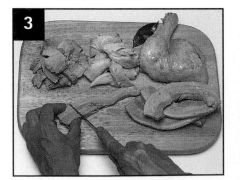

Authentic Guacamole

Guacamole is at its best when freshly made, with enough texture to really taste the avocado.
Serve as a sauce for anything Mexican, or dip into it with vegetable sticks or tortilla chips.

Serves 4

INGREDIENTS

1 ripe tomato
2 limes
2–3 ripe small to medium avocados, or 1–2 large ones
¼–½ onion, finely chopped

pinch of ground cumin
pinch of mild chilli powder
½–1 fresh green chillies, such as jalapeño or serrano, deseeded and finely chopped

1 tbsp finely chopped fresh coriander (cilantro) leaves, plus extra for garnishing
salt (optional)
tortilla chips, to serve (optional)

1 To skin the tomato, place in a heatproof bowl, pour boiling water over to cover and stand for 30 seconds. Drain and plunge into cold water. The skin will then slide off easily. Cut in half, deseed and chop the flesh.

2 Squeeze the juice from the limes into a small bowl. Cut one avocado in half around the stone (pit). Twist apart, then remove the stone (pit) with a knife. Carefully peel off the skin, dice the flesh and toss in the bowl of lime juice to prevent them from discolouring. Repeat with the remaining avocados. Mash the avocados coarsely.

3 Add the onion, tomato, cumin, chilli powder, chillies and fresh coriander (cilantro) to the avocados. If using as a dip for tortilla chips do not add salt. If using as a sauce, add salt to taste.

4 To serve the Guacamole as a dip, transfer to a serving dish, garnish with finely chopped fresh coriander (cilantro) and serve with tortilla chips.

COOK'S TIP

Avocados grow in abundance in Mexico, and Guacamole is used to add richness and flavour to all manner of dishes. Try spooning it into soups, especially chicken or seafood, or spreading it into sandwiches on thick crusty rolls (tortas). Spoon Guacamole over refried beans and melted cheese, then dig into it with salsa and crisp tortilla chips. Try Guacamole with roast chicken, or stir it into the pan juices for a rich avocado sauce.

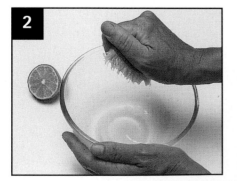

Roasted Cheese with Salsa

The combination of melting cheese and hot salsa is completely irresistible!
Called oueso fundito *in Mexico, it is often prepared on the barbecue (grill)*
to nibble on while you wait for the rest of the meal to cook.

Serves 4

INGREDIENTS

225 g/8 oz mozzarella, fresh pecorino or Mexican queso oaxaca

175 ml/6 fl oz/³/₄ cup Salsa Cruda (see page 96), or other good salsa

½–1 onion, finely chopped

8 tortillas, to serve

1 To warm the tortillas ready for serving, heat a non-stick frying pan (skillet), add a tortilla and heat through, sprinkling with a few drops of water as it heats. Wrap in kitchen foil to keep warm. Repeat with the other tortillas.

2 Cut chunks or slabs of cheese and arrange them in a shallow ovenproof dish or in individual dishes.

3 Spoon the salsa over the cheese to cover and place in either a preheated oven at 200°C/400°F/Gas Mark 6 or under a preheated grill (broiler). Cook until the cheese melts and bubbles, lightly browning in spots.

4 Sprinkle with chopped onion to taste and serve with the warmed tortillas for dipping. Serve immediately as the melted cheese turns stringy when cold and becomes difficult to eat.

COOK'S TIP

Queso oaxaca is the authentic cheese to use, but mozzarella or pecorino make excellent substitutes, since they produce the right effect when melted.

VARIATION

Use Salsa Verde (see page 102) in place of the red tomato salsa, and serve tortilla chips for dipping rather than soft corn tortillas.

Seafood Cocktail à la Veracruz

'Mariscos!' cry the signs in brightly painted colours along Mexico's beaches and sea fronts, wherever fresh seafood is served. This is a typical salad dish you will find on offer, full of spicy flavours.

Serves 6

INGREDIENTS

1 litre/1¾ pints/4 cups fish stock or water mixed with 1 fish stock cube
2 bay leaves
1 onion, chopped
3–5 garlic cloves, cut into big chunks
650 g/1 lb 8 oz mixed seafood, such as prawns (shrimp) in their shells,

scallops, squid rings, pieces of squid tentacles, etc
175 ml/6 fl oz/¾ cup tomato ketchup (catsup)
50 ml/2 fl oz/¼ cup Mexican hot sauce
generous pinch of ground cumin

6–8 tbsp chopped fresh coriander (cilantro)
4 tbsp lime juice, plus extra for tossing
salt
1 avocado, to garnish

1 Place stock in a pan and add the bay leaves, half the onion and all of the garlic. Bring to the boil, then simmer for about 10 minutes or until the onion and garlic are soft and the stock tastes flavourful.

2 Add the seafood in the order of the amount of cooking time required. Most small pieces of shellfish take a very short time to cook, and can be added together. Cook for 1 minute, then remove the pan from the heat and allow the seafood to finish cooking by standing in the cooling stock.

3 When the stock has cooled, remove the seafood from the stock with a slotted spoon. Shell the prawns (shrimp) and any other shellfish. Reserve the stock.

4 Combine the ketchup (catsup), hot sauce and cumin in a bowl, reserve a quarter of the sauce mixture for serving. Add the seafood to the bowl with the remaining onion, fresh coriander (cilantro), lime juice and about 225 ml/8 fl oz/1 cup of the reserved cooled fish stock. Stir carefully to mix and season with salt to taste.

5 Peel and stone the avocado, then dice or slice the flesh. Toss gently in lime juice to prevent discoloration.

6 Serve the seafood cocktail in individual bowls, garnished with the avocado, and topped with a spoonful of the reserved sauce.

Citrus-marinated Fish

Ceviche, as it is called in Mexican, is one of Mexico's classic dishes: raw fish, cured in a bath of citrus juices, chillies and aromatics. It must be made with the freshest fish to be sublime.

Serves 4

INGREDIENTS

450 g/1 lb white-fleshed fish fillets, cut into bite-sized chunks
juice of 6–8 limes
2–3 ripe flavourful tomatoes, diced

3 fresh green chillies, such as jalapeño or serrano, deseeded and thinly sliced
½ tsp dried oregano

80 ml/3 fl oz/⅓ cup extra-virgin olive oil
1 small onion, finely chopped
salt and pepper
2 tbsp chopped fresh coriander (cilantro)

1 Place the fish in a non-metallic dish, add the lime juice and mix well. Marinate in the refrigerator for 5 hours, or until the mixture looks opaque. Turn from time to time so that the lime juice permeates the fish.

2 An hour before serving, add the tomatoes, chillies, oregano, olive oil and onion, and then season with salt and pepper to taste.

3 About 15 minutes before serving, remove from the refrigerator so that the olive oil comes to room temperature. Serve the dish sprinkled with fresh coriander (cilantro).

COOK'S TIP

This dish makes an elegant starter served layered with rounds of crisp tortillas, like a stacked tostada. Or it makes a refreshing lunch, served piled up in halved avocados, surrounded by sliced mango, papaya or grapefruit.

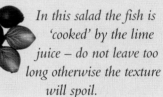

COOK'S TIP

In this salad the fish is 'cooked' by the lime juice – do not leave too long otherwise the texture will spoil.

VARIATION

Serve garnished with cooked marinated artichoke hearts, or drained artichokes from a can or jar.

Salpicon of Crab

This lightly spiced crab salad is a cooling treat for a hot day. Eat it with crisp tortilla chips, or wrapped in a tender warm corn tortilla.

Serves 4

INGREDIENTS

¼ red onion, chopped
½–1 fresh green chilli, deseeded and
  chopped
juice of ½ lime
1 tbsp cider or other fruit vinegar,
  such as raspberry

1 tbsp chopped fresh coriander
  (cilantro)
1 tbsp extra-virgin olive oil
225–350 g/8–12 oz fresh crab
  meat
lettuce leaves, to serve

TO GARNISH:
1 avocado
lime juice, for tossing
1–2 ripe tomatoes
3–5 radishes

1 Combine the onion, with the chilli, lime juice, vinegar, fresh coriander (cilantro) and olive oil. Add the crab meat and the ingredients toss lightly together.

2 To make the garnish, cut each avocado in half around the stone (pit). Twist apart, then remove the stone (pit) with a knife. Carefully peel off the skin and slice the flesh. Toss the avocado gently in lime juice to prevent discoloration.

3 Halve the tomatoes, then remove the cores and seeds. Dice the flesh. Slice the radishes thinly.

4 Arrange the crab salad on a bed of lettuce leaves, garnish with the avocado, tomatoes and radishes and serve at once.

VARIATION

For a toasted crab salad sandwich, split open a long roll or baguette and heap on crab salad. Top with a generous layer of cheese. Place the open roll under the grill (broiler) to melt the cheese. Spread the toasted plain side with a little mayonnaise and close the sandwich up. Cut and serve with salsa.

Pickled Cauliflower, Carrots & Chillies

In Mexican cantinas, these pickled vegetables are munched alongside a stack of warm buttered tortillas and washed down with glasses of chilled lager, or maybe a little shot of tequila and a wedge of lime.

Serves 6

INGREDIENTS

3 tbsp vegetable oil
1 onion, thinly sliced
5 garlic cloves, cut into slivers
3 carrots, thinly sliced
2 fresh green chillies, such as jalapeño or serrano, deseeded and cut into strips

1 small cauliflower, broken into florets or cut into bite-sized chunks
½ red (bell) pepper, cored, deseeded and diced or cut into strips
1 stalk celery, cut into bite-sized pieces

½ tsp oregano leaves
1 bay leaf
¼ tsp ground cumin
80 ml/3 fl oz/⅓ cup cider vinegar
salt and pepper

1 Heat the oil in a heavy-based frying pan (skillet) and lightly sauté the onion, garlic, carrots, chillies, cauliflower, red (bell) pepper and celery for about a minute until soft.

2 Add the oregano, bay leaf, cumin, cider vinegar and salt and pepper to taste. Add enough water to just cover the vegetables.

Cook for a further 5–10 minutes or just long enough for the vegetables to be tender but still firm to the bite.

3 Adjust the seasoning, adding more vinegar if needed. Leave to cool and serve as a relish. The mixture will keep for up to 2 weeks, if covered and stored in the refrigerator.

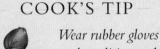

COOK'S TIP

Wear rubber gloves when slicing and deseeding fresh chillies and do not touch your eyes during preparation.

Cheese & Bean Quesadillas

These bite-sized rolls are made from flour tortillas filled with a scrumptious mixture of refried beans, melted cheese, fresh coriander (cilantro) and salsa.

Serves 4–6

INGREDIENTS

8 flour tortillas
½ quantity Mexican Refried Beans
(see page 146) or refried beans
(see page 144)

200 g/7 oz Cheddar cheese, grated
1 onion, chopped
½ bunch fresh coriander (cilantro)
leaves, chopped

1 quantity Salsa Cruda (see page 96)

1 First make the tortillas pliable, by warming them gently in a lightly greased non-stick frying pan (skillet).

2 Remove the tortillas from the pan and quickly spread with a layer of warm beans. Top each tortilla with grated cheese, onion, fresh coriander (cilantro) and a spoonful of salsa. Roll up tightly.

3 Just before serving, heat the non-stick frying pan (skillet) over a medium heat, sprinkling lightly with a drop or two of water. Add the tortilla rolls, cover the pan and heat through until the cheese melts. Allow to lightly brown, if wished.

4 Remove from the pan and slice each roll, on the diagonal, into about 4 bite-sized pieces. Serve the dish at once.

VARIATION

Top each tortilla with florets of lightly cooked broccoli or sautéed sliced wild mushrooms instead of the beans, for a more lightweight filling if you wish.

VARIATION

Cooked drained black beans can also be substituted for the refried beans – use with Chipotle Salsa (see page 98) instead of the Salsa Cruda for a subtle change of flavour.

COOK'S TIP

Flour tortillas can also be warmed in the microwave, but take care not to heat them for too long as they can become leathery.

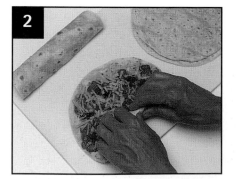

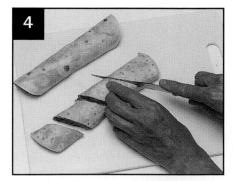

Chorizo & Artichoke Heart
Quesadillas

Ideal to serve with drinks, these bites are incredibly easy to make – simply top flat tortillas with a delicious filling, pop them under the grill (broiler), then serve in wedges.

Serves 4–6

INGREDIENTS

1 chorizo

1 large mild green chilli or green (bell) pepper (optional)

8–10 marinated artichoke hearts or canned artichoke hearts, drained and diced

4 corn tortillas, warmed

2 garlic cloves, finely chopped

350 g/12 oz cheese, grated

1 tomato, diced

2 spring onions (scallions), thinly sliced

1 tbsp chopped fresh coriander (cilantro)

1 Dice the chorizo sausage. Heat a heavy-based frying pan (skillet), add the chorizo and fry until it browns in places.

2 If using the mild chilli or (bell) pepper, place under a preheated hot grill (broiler) and grill (broil) for about 10 minutes, or until the skins are charred and the flesh softened. Place in a plastic bag, twist to seal and set aside for about 20 minutes. Carefully, remove the skins from the chilli or (bell) pepper with a knife, then deseed and chop.

3 Arrange the browned chorizo and artichoke hearts on the corn tortillas, then transfer half to a baking (cookie) sheet.

4 Sprinkle with the garlic, then the grated cheese. Place under a preheated hot grill (broiler) and grill (broil) until the cheese melts and sizzles. Repeat with the remaining tortillas.

5 Sprinkle the warm tortillas with the diced tomato, sliced spring onions (scallions), green chilli or (bell) pepper, if using, and chopped fresh coriander (cilantro). Cut into wedges and serve immediately.

Spicy Prawns (Shrimp) & Avocado on Crisp Tortilla Wedges

A winning combination of textures and flavours, spiced prawns (shrimp) and creamy avocado are served on crisply fried tortilla wedges to make an irresistible appetizer.

Serves 8–10

INGREDIENTS

500 g /1 2 oz lb cooked prawns
  (shrimp)
4 garlic cloves, finely chopped
½ tsp mild chilli powder
½ tsp ground cumin

juice of 1 lime
1 ripe tomato, diced
salt
6 corn tortillas
vegetable oil, for frying

2 avocados
200 ml/7 fl oz ¾ cup soured cream
mild chilli powder, to garnish

1 Place the prawns (shrimp) in a bowl with the garlic, chilli powder, cumin, lime juice and tomato. Add salt to taste and stir gently to mix. Chill for at least 4 hours or overnight to allow the flavours to mingle.

2 Cut the tortillas into wedges. Heat a little oil in a non-stick frying pan (skillet), add a batch of tortilla wedges and fry over a medium heat until crisp. Repeat with the remaining wedges and transfer to a serving platter.

3 Cut each avocado in half around the stone (pit). Twist apart, then remove the stone (pit) with a knife. Carefully peel off the skin and dice the flesh. Gently stir the avocado into the prawn (shrimp) mixture.

4 Top each tortilla wedge with a small mound of the prawn (shrimp) and avocado mixture. Finish with a dab of soured cream, garnish with a light sprinkling of chilli powder and serve at once while hot and crisp.

COOK'S TIP

For speed, you can use crisp corn tortillas (tostadas) or nacho chips (not too salty) instead of the corn tortillas.

VARIATION

Substitute diced mozzarella or mild fresh pecorino for the prawns and marinate for a few hours.

Black Bean Nachos

Packed with authentic Mexican flavours, this tasty black bean and cheese dip is fun to eat and will get any meal off to a good start! As an added bonus, it takes mere minutes to put together.

Serves 4

INGREDIENTS

225 g/8 oz/1 cup dried black beans, or canned black beans, drained
175–225 g/6–8 oz grated cheese, such as Cheddar, Fontina, pecorino, asiago, or a combination

about ¼ tsp cumin seeds or ground cumin
about 4 tbsp soured cream
thinly sliced pickled jalapeños (optional)

1 tbsp chopped fresh coriander (cilantro)
handful of shredded lettuce
tortilla chips, to serve

1 If using dried black beans, soak the beans overnight, then drain. Put in a pan, cover with water and bring to the boil. Boil for 10 minutes, then reduce the heat and simmer for about 1½ hours until tender. Drain well.

2 Spread the beans in a shallow ovenproof dish, then scatter the cheese over the top. Sprinkle with cumin, to taste.

3 Bake in a preheated oven at 190°C/375°F/Gas Mark 5 for 10–15 minutes or until the beans are cooked through and the cheese is bubbly and melted.

4 Remove the beans and cheese from the oven and spoon the soured cream on top. Add the jalapeños, if using, and sprinkle with fresh coriander (cilantro) and lettuce.

5 Arrange the tortilla chips around the beans, sticking them into the mixture. Serve the nachos at once.

VARIATION

To add a meaty flavour, spoon chopped and browned chorizo on top of the beans, before sprinkling over the cheese, and cook as in Step 3 – the combination is excellent. Finely chopped leftover cooked meat can also be added in this way.

Refried Bean Nachos

*A Mexican classic, refried beans and tortilla crisps are topped
with luscious melted cheese, salsa, and assorted toppings, to make an irresistible dip.
Perfect for an informal gathering!*

Serves 6–8

INGREDIENTS

400 g/14 oz refried beans
400 g/14 oz can pinto beans, drained
large pinch of ground cumin
large pinch of mild chilli powder
175 g/6 oz bag tortilla chips

225 g/8 oz grated cheese, such as
  Cheddar
salsa of your choice
1 avocado, stoned (pitted), diced
  and tossed with lime juice
½ small onion or 3–5 spring onions
  (scallions), chopped

2 ripe tomatoes, diced
handful of shredded lettuce
3–4 tbsp chopped fresh coriander
  (cilantro)
soured cream, to serve

1 Place the refried beans in a pan with the pinto beans, cumin and chilli powder. Add enough water to make a thick soup-like consistency, stirring gently so that the beans do not lose their texture.

2 Heat the bean mixture over a medium heat until hot, then reduce the heat and keep the mixture warm while you prepare the rest of the dish.

3 Arrange half the tortilla chips in the bottom of a flameproof casserole or gratin dish and cover with the bean mixture. Sprinkle with the cheese and bake in a preheated oven at 200°C/400°F/ Gas Mark 6 until the cheese melts.

4 Alternatively, place the casserole under the grill (broiler) and grill (broil) for 5–7 minutes or until the cheese melts and lightly sizzles in places.

5 Arrange on top of the melted cheese the salsa, avocado, onion, tomato, lettuce and fresh coriander (cilantro). Surround with the remaining tortilla chips and serve immediately with with soured cream.

VARIATION

Replace the soured cream with Greek yogurt as an alternative.

Sincronizadas

Once you've tried this Mexican version of a toasted ham and cheese sandwich, you'll never look back! Serve with a tangy salsa and Mexican beer to complete the snack.

Serves 6

INGREDIENTS

vegetable oil, for greasing
about 10 flour tortillas

about 500 g/1 lb 2 oz grated cheese
225 g/8 oz cooked ham, diced

salsa of your choice
soured cream with herbs, to serve

1 Lightly grease a non-stick frying pan (skillet). Off the heat, place 1 tortilla in the pan and top with a layer of cheese and ham. Generously spread salsa over another tortilla and place, salsa-side down, on top of the cheese and ham tortilla in the pan.

2 Place over a medium heat and cook until the cheese is melted and the base of the tortilla is golden brown.

3 Place a heatproof plate, upside-down, on top of the pan. Taking care to protect your hands, hold the plate firmly in place and carefully invert the pan

to turn the 'sandwich' out on to the plate.

4 Slide the 'sandwich' back into the frying pan (skillet) and cook until the underside of the tortilla is golden brown.

5 Remove from the pan and serve cut into wedges, accompanied with soured cream sprinkled with herbs.

VARIATIONS

For a vegetarian version, sauté 225 g/8 oz thinly sliced mushrooms in a little olive oil with a crushed garlic clove and use instead of the ham. Alternatively, lightly fry finely chopped garlic in a little oil, then add rinsed spinach leaves and cook until wilted; chop and substitute for the ham.

COOK'S TIP

Protect your hands with oven gloves (pot holders) when turning the tortillas on to the plate.

Tortas

Throughout Mexico you will find street vendors selling these substantial Mexican rolls.
Filled with all sorts of ingredients, they are 'Muy Delicioso'!
Make your own and vary the filling as you wish.

Serves 4

INGREDIENTS

4 crusty rolls, such as French rolls or
   bocadillos
melted butter or olive oil, for brushing
225 g/8 oz/1 cup refried beans
   (see page 144)
350 g/12 oz/1½ cups shredded
   cooked chicken, browned chorizo

pieces, sliced ham and cheese or
   any leftover cooked meat you have
   to hand
1 ripe tomato, sliced or diced
1 small onion, finely chopped
2 tbsp chopped fresh coriander
   (cilantro)

1 avocado, stoned (pitted), sliced and
   tossed with lime juice
4–6 tbsp soured cream or Greek
   yogurt
salsa of your choice
handful of shredded lettuce

1 Cut the rolls in half and remove a little of the crumb to make space for the filling.

2 Brush the outside and inside of the rolls with butter or oil and toast, on both sides, on a hot griddle or frying pan (skillet) for a few minutes until crisp. Alternatively, place in a preheated oven at 200°C/400°F/Gas Mark 6 until lightly toasted.

3 Meanwhile, place the beans in a pan with a tiny amount of water and heat through gently.

4 When the rolls are heated, spread one half of each roll generously with the beans, then top with a layer of cooked meat. Top with tomato, onion, fresh coriander (cilantro) and avocado.

5 Generously spread soured cream or yogurt on to the other side of each roll. Drizzle the salsa over the filling, add a little shredded lettuce, then sandwich the two sides of each roll together; press tightly. Serve immediately.

VARIATION

Add any Mexican sauce, such as Chile Verde (see page 204), to the meat filling to vary the flavour.

Molletes

Molletes are crusty rolls stuffed with hot melted beans and cheese, then garnished with a tangy hot salsa. In this version, a spicy shredded cabbage salad adds extra crunch to the snacks.

Serves 4

INGREDIENTS

4 bread rolls
1 tbsp vegetable oil, plus extra for brushing
400 g/14 oz can refried beans
1 onion, chopped
3 garlic cloves, chopped

3 slices bacon, cut into small pieces, or about 80 g/3 oz spicy chorizo, diced
225 g/8 oz diced fresh or canned tomatoes
¼–½ tsp ground cumin
250 g/9 oz grated cheese

CABBAGE SALAD:
½ cabbage, thinly sliced
2 tbsp sliced pickled jalapeños
1 tbsp extra-virgin olive oil
3 tbsp cider vinegar
¼ tsp dried oregano
salt and pepper

1 Cut the rolls in half and remove a little of the crumb to make space for the filling.

2 To make the cabbage salad, combine the cabbage with the jalapeños, olive oil and vinegar. Season with salt, pepper and oregano. Set aside.

3 Brush the rolls all over with oil. Arrange on a baking (cookie) sheet and toast in a preheated oven at 200°C/400°F/ Gas Mark 6 oven for 10–15 minutes until the rolls are crisp and light golden.

4 Meanwhile, place the beans in a pan and heat through gently with enough water to thin them to a smooth paste.

5 Heat 1 tablespoon of the oil in a frying pan (skillet). Add the onion, garlic and bacon or chorizo and cook until the bacon or chorizo is browned and the onion softened. Add the tomatoes and simmer, stirring, until they break down to form a thick sauce.

6 Add the beans to the frying pan (skillet) and stir to combine with the onion mixture. Stir in the cumin, to taste. Set aside.

7 Remove the rolls from the oven: keep the oven on. Fill the rolls with the warm bean mixture, then top with the cheese and close up tightly. Return to the baking (cookie) sheet and heat through in the oven until the cheese melts.

8 Open the rolls up and spoon in a little cabbage salad. Serve.

Spicy-sweet Meat Empanadas

This is a great make-ahead appetizer as it can be frozen for a month, then just popped into the oven at the last moment – will still taste marvellous!

Serves 4–6

INGREDIENTS

350 g/12 oz puff pastry
plain (all-purpose) flour, for dusting
1 quantity Spicy Beef Filling
(see page 198)

1 egg yolk, beaten with 1–2 tbsp
water

TO SERVE:
green olives
mixed chillies

1 Roll out the puff pastry into a thin layer on a lightly floured surface. Using a 15 cm/6 inch cutter, cut the pastry into 8 rounded shapes.

2 Place a tablespoon or two of the filling in the middle of one round.

3 Brush the edge of the pastry with beaten egg, then fold in half and press the edges together to seal.

4 Press the tines of a fork along the sealed edges of the pastry to make the seal more secure.

Prick the top of the empanada with the fork, then place on a baking (cookie) sheet. Brush with beaten egg. Repeat this process with the remaining pastry rounds and filling.

5 Bake the empanadas in a preheated oven at 190°C/375°F/Gas Mark 5 for 15–25 minutes or until a light golden brown on the outside and hot in the middle.

6 Serve immediately, hot and sizzling from the oven, accompanied by a bowl of olives and chillies.

VARIATION

For chicken empanadas, replace the Spicy Beef Filling with diced cooked chicken, flavoured with some mild chilli sauce.

VARIATION

For vegetarian empanadas, replace the filling with a mixture of diced Gouda or Cheddar cheese, chopped onion, fresh coriander (cilantro), cumin seeds and sliced pimiento-stuffed green olives. Fill and bake as described.

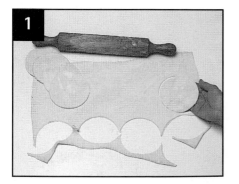

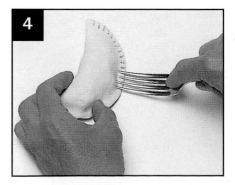

Masa Tartlets
with Beans & Avocado

*Packed with Mexican flavours, these little golden tartlets make a colourful start to a
meal or a tasty light lunch, when served with mixed salad leaves.*

Serves 4

INGREDIENTS

8–10 tbsp masa harina
3 tbsp plain (all-purpose) flour
pinch of baking powder
about 225 ml/8 fl oz/1 cup warm
  water
vegetable oil, for frying

225 g/8 oz/1 cup pinto beans or
  refried beans, heated through
1 avocado, stoned (pitted), sliced and
  tossed with lime juice
80 g/3 oz queso fresco or fresh
  cream cheese or crumbled feta

salsa of your choice
2 spring onions, thinly sliced

TO GARNISH:
fresh flat-leaf parsley sprigs
lemon wedges

1 Mix the masa harina with the
plain (all-purpose) flour and
baking powder in a bowl, then
mix in enough warm water to
make a firm yet moist dough.

2 Pinch off about a walnut-
sized piece of dough and,
using your fingers, shape into a
tiny tartlet shape, pressing and
pinching to make it as thin as
possible without falling apart.
Repeat with the remaining dough.

3 Heat a layer of oil in a deep
frying pan (skillet) until it is
smoking. Add a batch of tartlets to
the hot oil and fry, spooning the
hot fat into the centre of the
tartlets and turning once, until
golden on all sides.

4 Using a slotted spoon,
remove the tartlets from the
hot oil and drain on paper towels.
Place on a baking (cookie) sheet
and keep warm in the oven on a

low temperature, while cooking
the remaining tartlets.

5 To serve, fill each tartlet shell
with the warmed beans,
avocado, cheese, salsa and spring
onions (scallions). Garnish with
parsley and lemon wedges and
serve at once.

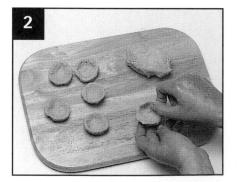

Salads, Side & Dishes Sauces

Salads of crisp raw vegetables and fruits, often eaten piled on top of richer savoury cooked dishes, such as enchiladas or barbecued (grilled) food, are full of strong fresh flavour and rich with vitamins, too. Pomegranate, papaya and tangy citrus fruits are combined with avocado or red (bell) peppers to stunning effect.

For heartier salads, Steak, Avocado Bean Salad is a substantial dish, while summer squash and chorizo, two popular ingredients in Mexico, make the basis for a great lunch-time snack.

For a delicious side dish, try a gratin of potatoes lavished with mild red chilli sauce, layered with goats' cheese and baked until lightly crusty. Or try fragrant Roasted Green Chillies in Cumin-garlic Cream – a classic accompaniment to all sorts of main courses.

Sauces for topping meat and fish or for filling tortillas are on offer in this chapter, too – the Quick Tomato Sauce can be used for all manner of dishes, while Hot Sauce of Dried Chillies will add a hotnesss that is the very essence of Mexican cuisine. Mole Poblano, the classic sauce of chillies and chocolate, is not to be missed.

Papaya, Avocado & Red (Bell) Pepper Salad

This colourful and refreshing salad, with its sweet and spicy flavours, is the perfect foil to a meaty main dish, and is particularly good with barbecued (grilled) food.

Serves 4–6

INGREDIENTS

200 g/7 oz mixed green salad leaves
2–3 spring onions (scallions), chopped
3–4 tbsp chopped fresh coriander
 (cilantro)
1 small papaya
2 red (bell) peppers
1 avocado

1 tbsp lime juice
3–4 tbsp pumpkin seeds, preferably
 toasted (optional)

DRESSING:
juice of 1 lime
large pinch of paprika

large pinch of ground cumin
large pinch of sugar
1 garlic clove, finely chopped
4 tbsp extra-virgin olive oil
dash of white wine vinegar (optional)
salt

1 Combine the salad leaves with the spring onions (scallions) and coriander (cilantro). Mix well, then transfer the salad to a large serving dish.

2 Cut the papaya in half and scoop out the seeds with a spoon. Cut into quarters, remove the peel and slice the flesh. Arrange on top of the salad leaves. Cut the (bell) peppers in half,

remove the cores and seeds, then slice thinly. Add the peppers to the salad leaves.

3 Cut the avocado in half around the stone (pit). Twist apart, then remove the stone (pit) with a knife. Carefully peel off the skin, dice the flesh and toss in lime juice to prevent the avocado from discolouring. Add to the other salad ingredients.

4 To make the dressing, whisk together the lime juice, paprika, ground cumin, sugar, garlic and olive oil. Add salt to suit your taste.

5 Pour the dressing over the salad and toss lightly, adding a dash of wine vinegar if a flavour with more 'bite' is preferred. Sprinkle with the toasted pumpkin seeds, if using.

Green Bean Salad
with Feta Cheese

*This fresh-tasting salad is flavoured with fresh coriander (cilantro),
a herb used widely in Mexican cooking.*

Serves 4

INGREDIENTS

350 g/12 oz green beans, topped and
tailed
1 red onion, chopped
3–4 tbsp chopped fresh coriander
(cilantro)

2 radishes, thinly sliced
75 g/2 ¾ oz feta cheese, crumbled
1 tsp chopped fresh oregano or
½ tsp dried
2 tbsp red wine or fruit vinegar

80 ml/3 fl oz/⅓ cup extra-virgin olive
oil
3 ripe tomatoes, cut into wedges
pepper

1 Bring about 5 cm/2 inches water to the boil in the bottom of a steamer. Add the beans to the top part of the steamer, cover and steam for about 5 minutes until just tender.

2 Put the beans in a bowl and add the onion, coriander (cilantro), radishes and feta cheese.

3 Sprinkle the oregano over the salad, then grind pepper over to taste. Mix the vinegar and olive oil together and pour over the salad. Toss gently to mix well.

4 Transfer to a serving platter, surround with the tomato wedges and serve at once, or chill until ready to serve.

VARIATION

This recipe is also delicious made with nopales, or edible cactus, which is used as a vegetable in Mexican cooking. It is available in specialist stores in cans or jars. Simply drain the cactus, then slice and use instead of the green beans, missing out Step 1. When using cactus, replace the feta cheese with 1–2 chopped hard-boiled (hard-cooked) eggs.

Citrus Salad
with Pomegranate & Avocado

*A salad like this reminds one of how much Mexico and the Mediterranean
share in terms of sunny flavours and ingredients.*

Serves 4

INGREDIENTS

1 large pomegranate
1 grapefruit
2 sweet oranges
finely grated rind of ½ lime
1–2 garlic cloves, finely chopped
3 tbsp red wine vinegar

juice of 2 limes
½ tsp sugar
¼ tsp dry mustard
4–5 tbsp extra-virgin olive oil
1 head red leafy lettuce, such as
   oakleaf, washed and dried

1 avocado, stoned (pitted), diced and
   tossed with a little lime juice
salt and pepper
½ red onion, thinly sliced, to garnish

1 Cut the pomegranate into quarters, then press back the outer skin to push out the seeds into a bowl.

2 Using a sharp knife, cut a slice off the top and bottom of the grapefruit, then remove the peel and pith, cutting downwards. Cut out the segments from between the membranes, then add to the pomegranate.

3 Finely grate the rind of half an orange and set aside. Using a sharp knife, cut a slice off the top and bottom of both oranges, then remove the peel and pith, cutting downwards and taking care to retain the shape of the oranges. Slice horizontally into slices, then cut into quarters. Add the oranges to the pomegranate and grapefruit and stir to mix well.

4 Combine the reserved orange rind with the lime rind, garlic, vinegar, lime juice, sugar and mustard. Season with salt and pepper, then whisk in the olive oil.

5 Place the lettuce leaves in a serving bowl, then top with the citrus mixture and the avocado. Pour over the dressing and toss gently. Garnish with the onion rings and serve at once.

Courgettes (Zucchini) & Tomatoes with Green Chilli Vinaigrette

Lightly cooked courgettes (zucchini) are mixed with ripe, juicy tomatoes and dressed with a chilli vinaigrette to create a perfect side salad for a summer lunch or supper.

Serves 4–6

INGREDIENTS

1 large fresh mild green chilli, or a combination of 1 green (bell) pepper and ½–1 fresh green chilli
4 courgettes (zucchini), sliced

2–3 garlic cloves, finely chopped
pinch sugar
¼ tsp ground cumin
2 tbsp white wine vinegar

4 tbsp extra-virgin olive oil
2–3 tbsp coriander (cilantro)
4 ripe tomatoes, diced or sliced
salt and pepper

1 Roast the mild chilli, or the combination of the green (bell) pepper and chilli, in a heavy-based ungreased frying pan (skillet) or under a preheated grill (broiler) until the skin is charred. Place in a plastic bag, twist to seal well and leave the mixture to stand for 20 minutes.

2 Peel the skin from the chilli and (bell) pepper, if using, then remove the seeds and slice the flesh. Set aside.

3 Bring about 5 cm/2 inches water to the boil in the bottom of a steamer. Add the courgettes (zucchini) to the top part of the steamer, cover and steam for about 5 minutes until just tender.

4 Meanwhile, thoroughly combine the garlic, sugar, cumin, vinegar, olive oil and coriander (cilantro) in a bowl. Stir in the chilli and (bell) pepper, if using, then season with salt and pepper to taste.

5 Arrange the courgettes (zucchini) and tomatoes in a serving bowl or on a platter and spoon over the chilli dressing. Toss gently, if wished, and serve.

VARIATION

Add 225 g/8oz cooked peeled prawns (shrimp) to the courgettes (zucchini) and tomatoes, then coat with the dressing as in Step 5.

Steak, Avocado & Bean Salad

The Californian influence on Mexican food is evident in this big, hearty salad.
Packed with delicious ingredients, this fantastic dish is a meal in itself.

Serves 4

INGREDIENTS

350 g/12 oz tender steak, such as
   sirloin or filet
4 garlic cloves, chopped
juice of 1 lime
4 tbsp extra-virgin olive oil
1 tbsp white or red wine vinegar
¼ tsp mild chilli powder
¼ tsp ground cumin
½ tsp paprika

pinch of sugar (optional)
5 spring onions (scallions), thinly
   sliced
about 200 g/7 oz crisp lettuce leaves,
   such as cos (romaine), or mixed
   herb leaves
400 g/14 oz can pinto, black or red
   kidney beans, drained
1 avocado, stoned (pitted), sliced and

tossed with a little lime juice
2 ripe tomatoes, diced
¼ fresh green or red chilli, chopped
3 tbsp chopped fresh coriander
   (cilantro)
225 g/8 oz can sweetcorn, drained
generous handful of crisp tortilla
   chips, broken into pieces
salt and pepper

1 Place the steak in a non-metallic dish with the garlic and half the lime and olive oil. Season with salt and pepper, then leave to marinate.

2 To make the dressing, combine the remaining lime juice and olive oil with the vinegar, chilli powder, cumin and paprika. Add a pinch of sugar to taste. Set aside.

3 Pan fry the steak, or cook under a preheated grill (broiler), until browned on the outside and cooked to your liking in the middle. Remove from the pan, cut into strips and reserve; keep warm or allow to cool.

4 Toss the spring onions (scallions) with the lettuce and arrange on a serving platter. Pour about half the dressing over the leaves, then arrange the sweetcorn, beans, avocado and tomatoes over the top. Sprinkle with the chilli and coriander (cilantro).

5 Arrange the steak and the tortilla chips on top, pour over the rest of the dressing, and serve at once.

Courgettes (Zucchini) & Summer Squash with Chorizo

The spicy richness of chorizo marries well with courgettes (zucchini) and squash, giving them a real flavour lift.

Serves 4

INGREDIENTS

2 courgettes (zucchini), thinly sliced
2 yellow summer squash, thinly sliced
2 fresh chorizo sausages, diced or
  sliced

3 garlic cloves, finely chopped
juice of ½–1 lime
1–2 tbsp chopped fresh coriander
  (cilantro)

salt and pepper

1 Cook the courgettes (zucchini) and summer squash in boiling salted water for 3–4 minutes until they are just tender, then drain well.

2 Brown the chorizo in a heavy-based frying pan (skillet), stirring with a spoon to break up into pieces. Pour off any excess fat from the browned chorizo, then add the garlic and blanched courgettes (zucchini) and summer squash. Cook for a few minutes, stirring gently, to combine the flavours.

3 Stir in the lime juice, to taste. Season with salt and pepper and serve at once sprinkled with chopped coriander (cilantro).

COOK'S TIP

Mild in flavour and ideal for combining with spicy meats, squash is a favourite Mexican vegetable. If wished, this dish can be prepared with squash only – yellow pattypans would be ideal.

VARIATION

For variety, why not use the rather more exotic squash known as chayote or cho-cho, which is indigenous to Mexico. This is pear-shaped and is usually pale green, with a corrugated skin. To prepare, simply peel and slice, then blanch as in Step 1, cooking for a few minutes longer. Use with yellow-coloured courgettes (zucchini) for visual appeal.

Summer Squash with Green Chillies, Tomatoes & Sweetcorn

Garlicky butter and a hint of chilli flavour this summertime vegetable pot of squash and sweetcorn. Serve alongside almost any meaty main course, especially a roasted chicken; good, too with Fajitas.

Serves 4–6

INGREDIENTS

2 corn-on-the-cobs

2 small courgettes (zucchini) or other green summer squash, such as pattypan, cubed or sliced

2 small yellow summer squash, cubed or sliced

2 tbsp butter

3 garlic cloves, finely chopped

3–4 large, ripe flavourful tomatoes, diced

several pinches of mild chilli powder

several pinches of ground cumin

½ fresh green chilli, such as jalapeño, deseeded and chopped

pinch of sugar

salt and pepper

1 Bring about 5 cm/2 inches water to the boil in the bottom of a steamer. Add the corn-on-the-cobs, courgettes (zucchini) and summer squash to the top part of the steamer, cover and steam for about 3 minutes depending on their maturity and freshness. Alternatively, blanch in boiling salted water for about 3 minutes, then drain. Set aside until cool enough to handle.

2 Using a large knife, slice the corn kernels off the cobs and set aside.

3 Melt the butter in a heavy-based frying pan (skillet). Add the garlic and cook for 1 minute to soften. Add the tomatoes, chilli powder, ground cumin, green chilli and sugar to taste. Season with salt and pepper to taste and cook for a few minutes or until the flavours have mingled.

4 Add the corn kernels, courgettes (zucchini) and squash. Cook for 2 minutes, stirring, to warm through. Serve at once.

VARIATION

Any leftovers will make a good base for a lovely summer soup. Simply thin with lots of stock and freshen up with chopped herbs.

Potatoes in Green Sauce

*Earthy potatoes, served in the tangy spicy tomatillo sauce and topped with spring onions (scallions)
and soured cream, are delicious either as a side dish with simmered or braised meat,
or as a vegetarian main course.*

Serves 6

INGREDIENTS

1 kg/2 lb 4 oz small waxy potatoes,
  peeled
1 onion, halved and unpeeled
8 garlic cloves, unpeeled
1 fresh green chilli
8 tomatillos, outer husks removed, or
  small tart tomatoes

225 ml/8 fl oz/1 cup chicken,
  meat or vegetable stock,
  preferably homemade
½ tsp ground cumin
1 sprig fresh thyme or generous
  pinch dried
1 sprig fresh oregano or generous
  pinch dried

2 tbsp vegetable or extra-virgin
  olive oil
1 bunch fresh coriander (cilantro),
  chopped
1 courgette (zucchini), roughly
  chopped
salt

1 Put the potatoes in a pan of salted water. Bring to the boil and cook for about 15 minutes or until almost tender. Do not over-cook them. Drain and set aside.

2 Lightly char the onion, garlic, chilli and tomatillos or tomatoes in a heavy-based ungreased frying pan (skillet). Set aside, and when cool enough to handle, peel and chop the onion, garlic and chilli; chop the tomatillos or tomatoes. Put in a blender or food processor with half the stock and process to form a purée. Add the cumin, thyme and oregano.

3 Heat the oil in the heavy-based frying pan (skillet). Add the purée and cook for 5 minutes, stirring, to reduce slightly and concentrate the flavours.

4 Add the potatoes and courgette (zucchini) to the purée and pour in the rest of the stock. Add about half the coriander (cilantro) and cook for a further 5 minutes or until the courgettes (zucchini) tender.

5 Transfer to a serving bowl and serve sprinkled with the remaining chopped coriander (cilantro) to garnish.

Potatoes with Goat's Cheese & Chipotle Cream

This makes a luscious side dish to serve with meat, or a satisfying vegetarian main course. Goat's cheese is a traditional food of Mexico, and is enjoying great renewed popularity.

Serves 4

INGREDIENTS

1.25 kg/2 lb 12 oz baking potatoes, peeled and cut into chunks
pinch of salt
pinch of sugar
200 ml/7 fl oz/³⁄₄ cup crème fraîche
120 ml/4 fl oz/½ cup vegetable or chicken stock

3 garlic cloves, finely chopped
a few shakes of bottled chipotle salsa, or ½ dried chipotle, reconstituted (see page 100), deseeded and thinly sliced
225 g/8 oz goat's cheese, sliced

175 g/6 oz mozzarella or Cheddar cheese, grated
50 g/³⁄₄ oz Parmesan or pecorino cheese, grated
salt

1 Put the potatoes in a pan of water with the salt and sugar. Bring to the boil and cook for about 10 minutes until they are half cooked.

2 Combine the crème fraîche with the stock, garlic and the chipotle salsa.

3 Arrange half the potatoes in a casserole. Pour half the crème fraîche sauce over the potatoes and cover with the goat's cheese. Top with the remaining potatoes and the sauce.

4 Sprinkle with the grated mozzarella or Cheddar cheese, then with either the grated Parmesan or pecorino.

5 Bake in a preheated oven at 180°C/350°F/Gas Mark 4 until the potatoes are tender and the cheese topping is lightly golden and crisped in places. Serve at once.

Roasted Green Chillies in Cumin-garlic Cream

Roasted mild green chillies are delicious simmered with cumin-scented cream.
It's important not to make this too hot, otherwise the fragrant aromas will be overpowered.

Serves 4–6

INGREDIENTS

4 large fresh mild green chillies, such as anaheim or poblano, or a combination of 4 green (bell) peppers and 2 jalapeños
2 tbsp butter

1 onion, finely chopped
3 garlic cloves, finely chopped
¼ tsp ground cumin
225 ml/8 fl oz/1 cup single (light) cream

225 ml/8 fl oz/1 cup chicken or vegetable stock
salt and pepper
1 lime, halved, to serve

1 Roast the mild chillies, or the combination of (bell) peppers and jalapeños, in a heavy-based ungreased frying pan (skillet) or under a preheated grill (broiler) until the skins are charred. Place in a plastic bag, twist to seal well and leave to stand for 20 minutes to allow the skins to loosen.

2 Remove the seeds from the chillies and (bell) peppers, if using, and peel off the skins. Slice the flesh. Set aside.

3 Melt the butter in a large frying pan (skillet), add the onion and garlic and sauté for about 3 minutes until softened. Sprinkle with the cumin and season with salt and pepper to your taste.

4 Stir in the sliced chillies and pour in the cream and stock. Cook over a medium heat, stirring, until the liquid reduces in volume and forms a richly flavoured sauce.

5 Transfer to a serving dish and serve warm, squeezing over lime juice at the last minute.

VARIATION

Add an equal amount of sweetcorn with the chillies – they add a delicious sweetness to the dish.

Quick Tomato Sauce

Simple to make, this versatile sauce is not only a great accompaniment for barbecued (grilled) meat and fish, but also invaluable for baked tortilla dishes and taco fillings.

Serves 4–6

INGREDIENTS

2 tbsp vegetable or olive oil
1 onion, thinly sliced
5 garlic cloves, thinly sliced

400 g/14 oz can tomatoes, diced,
  plus their juices, or 600 g/1 lb 5 oz
  fresh diced tomatoes
several shakes of mild chilli powder

350 ml/12 fl oz/1½ cups vegetable
  or chicken stock
salt and pepper
pinch of sugar (optional)

1 Heat the oil in a large frying pan (skillet). Add the onion and garlic and cook, stirring, until just softened.

2 Add the tomatoes, chilli powder to taste and the vegetable or chicken stock. Cook over a medium-high heat for about 10 minutes or until the tomatoes have reduced slightly and the flavour of the sauce is more concentrated.

3 Season the sauce with salt, pepper and sugar to taste and serve the dish warm.

COOK'S TIP

If using fresh tomatoes for this sauce, make sure they are very ripe and flavourful. Skin and deseed fresh tomatoes before dicing.

COOK'S TIP

The sauce will keep covered in the refrigerator for up to 3 days.

VARIATION

For a hotter kick, add a ¹/₂ teaspoon of finely chopped fresh chilli with the onion.

Hot Tomato Sauce

This tangy sauce is excellent with crispy tortillas and tostadas, or with grilled (broiled) or fried fish. Try it with fish and chips for a change!

Serves 4

INGREDIENTS

2–3 fresh green chillies, such as
   jalapeño or serrano
225 g/8 oz canned chopped
   tomatoes
1 spring onion (scallion), thinly
   sliced

2 garlic cloves, chopped
2–3 tbsp cider vinegar
50–80 ml/2–3 fl oz/$^1/_4$–$^1/_3$
   cup water
large pinch of dried oregano
large pinch of ground cumin

large pinch of sugar
large pinch of salt

1 Slice the chillies open,
   remove the seeds if wished,
then chop the chillies.

2 Put the chillies in a blender
   or food processor together
with the tomatoes, spring onion
(scallion), garlic, vinegar, water,
oregano, cumin, sugar and salt.
Process until smooth.

3 Adjust the seasoning and chill
   until ready to serve. The
sauce will keep for up to a week,
covered, in the refrigerator.

COOK'S TIP

*If you have sensitive skin, it may
be advisable to wear rubber gloves
when preparing chillies, as the oil
in the seeds and flesh can cause
irritation. Make sure that you do
not touch your eyes when handling
cut chillies.*

Mild Red Chilli Sauce

This milder sauce is ideal for enchiladas and stewed meat. Keep some stashed in your freezer at all times, for an instant hit of Mexico!

Makes about 350 ml/12 fl oz/1½ cups

INGREDIENTS

5 large fresh mild chillies, such as New Mexico or ancho
450 ml/16 fl oz /2 cups vegetable or chicken stock

1 tbsp masa harina or 1 crumbled corn tortilla, puréed with enough water to make a thin paste
large pinch of ground cumin

1–2 garlic cloves, finely chopped
juice of 1 lime
salt

1 Using metal tongs, roast each chilli over an open flame until the colour darkens on all sides. Alternatively, place the chillies under a preheated grill (broiler), turning them frequently.

2 Put the chillies in a bowl and pour boiling water over them. Cover and leave the chillies to cool.

3 Meanwhile, put the stock in a pan and bring to a simmer.

4 When the chillies have cooled and are swelled up and softened, remove from the water with a slotted spoon. Remove the seeds from the chillies, then cut or tear the flesh into pieces and place in a blender or food processor. Process to form a purée, then mix in the hot stock.

5 Put the chilli and stock mixture in a pan. Add the masa harina or puréed tortilla, cumin, garlic and lime juice. Bring to the boil and cook for a few

minutes, stirring, until the sauce has thickened. Adjust the seasoning and serve.

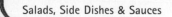

Hot Sauce
of Dried Chillies

*Perfect for adding a splash of authentic hot Mexican
flavour to a dish, this sauce will prove to be a handy standby.*

Makes about 225 ml/8 fl oz/1 cup

INGREDIENTS

10 dried arbol chillies, stems removed
(see Cook's Tip)

225 ml/8 fl oz/1 cup cider or white
wine vinegar

½ tsp salt

1 Place the dried arbol chillies
in a mortar and crush finely
with a pestle.

2 Put the cider or white wine
vinegar in a pan and add the
crushed chillies and salt. Stir to
combine, then bring the liquid to
the boil.

3 Remove from the heat and
leave to cool completely to
allow the flavours to infuse. Pour
into a bowl and serve. The sauce
will keep for up to a month, if
covered and kept in the
refrigerator.

COOK'S TIP

*Arbol are dried long hot red
chillies, with a dusty heat
that is reminiscent of the
Mexican desert. If arbol
chillies are not available, use any
hot dried chilli, or chilli flakes,
such as cayenne.*

COOK'S TIP

*Hot sauce can be bottled by
pouring into sterilized jars and
treating it as you would any
long–keeping jam, jelly or preserve.*

Mole Poblano

This great Mexican celebration dish, ladled out at village fiestas, birthday parties,
baptisms and weddings, is known for its unusual combination of chillies and chocolate.

Serves 8–10

INGREDIENTS

3 mulato chillies

3 mild ancho chillies

5–6 New Mexico or California chillies

1 onion, chopped

5 garlic cloves, chopped

450 g/1 lb ripe tomatoes

2 tortillas, preferably stale, cut into
   small pieces

pinch of cloves

pinch of fennel seeds

⅛ tsp each ground cinnamon,
coriander and cumin

3 tbsp lightly toasted sesame seeds or
   tahini

3 tbsp flaked or coarsely ground
   blanched almonds

2 tbsp raisins

1 tbsp peanut butter (optional)

450 ml/16 fl oz/2 cups chicken stock

3–4 tbsp grated semi-sweet
   chocolate, plus extra for garnishing

2 tbsp mild chilli powder

3 tbsp vegetable oil

about 1 tbsp lime juice

salt and pepper

1 Using metal tongs, toast each chilli over an open flame for a few seconds until the colour darkens. Alternatively, roast in an ungreased frying pan (skillet) over a medium heat, turning constantly, for about 30 seconds.

2 Place the toasted chillies in a bowl or a pan and pour boiling water over to cover. Cover with a lid and leave to soften for at least one hour or overnight. Once or twice lift the lid and rearrange the chillies so that they soak evenly.

3 Remove the softened chillies with a slotted spoon. Discard the stems and seeds and cut the flesh into pieces. Place in a blender.

4 Add the onion, garlic, tomatoes, tortillas, cloves, fennel seeds, cinnamon, coriander, cumin, sesame seeds, almonds, raisins and peanut butter if using, then process to combine. With the motor running, add enough stock through the feed tube to make a smooth paste. Stir in the remaining stock, chocolate and chilli powder.

5 Heat the oil in a heavy-based pan until it is smoking, then pour in the mole mixture. It will splatter and pop as it hits the hot oil. Cook for about 10 minutes, stirring occasionally to prevent it from burning.

6 Season with salt, pepper and lime juice, garnish with grated chocolate and serve.

Mole Verde

Moles are purées and, depending on the ingredients, they vary in colour from yellow and green to chocolate brown. This green mole is a speciality of Jalisco. Serve with either warm corn tortillas or unfilled tamales.

Serves 4-6

INGREDIENTS

250 g/9 oz toasted pumpkin seeds
1 litre/1¾ pints/4 cups chicken stock
several pinches of ground cloves
8-10 tomatillos, diced or use 225ml/
   8 fl oz/1 cup mild tomatillo salsa
½ onion, chopped

½ fresh green chilli, deseeded and
   diced
3 garlic cloves, chopped
½ tsp fresh thyme leaves
½ tsp fresh marjoram leaves
3 tbsp lard or vegetable oil
3 bay leaves

4 tbsp chopped fresh coriander
   (cilantro)
salt and pepper
fresh green chilli slices, to garnish

1 Grind the toasted pumpkin seeds in a food processor. Add half the chicken stock, the cloves, tomatillos, onion, chilli, garlic, thyme and marjoram and blend to a purée.

2 Heat the lard or oil in a heavy-based frying pan and add the puréed pumpkin seed mixture and the bay leaves. Cook over a medium-high heat for about 5 minutes until the mixture has began to thicken.

3 Remove from the heat and add the rest of the stock and the coriander (cilantro). Return the pan to the heat and cook until the sauce thickens, then remove from the heat.

4 Remove the bay leaves and process the sauce until completley smooth again. Add salt and pepper to taste.

5 Transfer to a bowl, garnish with chilli and serve.

VARIATION

Make a tamale dough (see page 138) and poach in the mole as dumplings, making a filling snack.

Salsa, Tortillas, & Beans Rice

Salsas appear on every table of every corner of Mexico, raw, cooked, chopped, chunky, smooth, spicy, mild or fiery. They are what adds interest to often simple fare. What's more, they are delicious and good for you too, as long as you don't burn your tongue. In this recipe you'll find the full range from sizzling Salsa Verde to powerful and smoky Chipotle Salsa and cooling Fresh Pineapple Salsa.

Tortillas are not only the bread of Mexico, they are also its knives and forks: break off a piece of tortilla, wrap it up in whatever you are eating, and you have an instant taco, no eating utensils needed. The variety of dishes made with tortillas in this chapter, range from fish-filled tacos and tostadas topped with chicken and green salsa, to burritos filled with lamb and black beans.

In Mexico, beans and rice are eaten every day, for nearly every meal: a pot of beans is almost always simmering on the back of nearly every stove in the land, and great pots of rice are cooked using the stock of simmering meats. Discover how to make Mexico's famous dish of refried beans, and learn the secret of Green Rice – a delicious dish, flavoured with roasted onions, garlic, chilli and plenty of coriander (cilantro).

If you ate nothing but salsas, dishes of tortillas, beans and rice, you would be eating the very soul of Mexico.

Two Classic Salsas

A Mexican meal is not complete without an accompanying salsa. These two traditional salsas are ideal for seasoning any dish, from filled tortillas to grilled (broiled) meat – they add a spicy hotness that is the very essence of Mexican cooking.

Serves 4–6

INGREDIENTS

JALAPEÑO SALSA:
1 onion, finely chopped
2–3 garlic cloves, finely chopped
4–6 tbsp coarsely chopped pickled
   jalapeño chillies
juice of ½ lemon
about ¼ tsp ground cumin
salt

SALSA CRUDA:
6–8 ripe tomatoes, finely chopped
about 100 ml/3½ fl oz/scant ½ cup
   tomato juice
3–4 garlic cloves, finely chopped
½–1 bunch fresh coriander (cilantro)
   leaves, coarsely chopped
pinch of sugar

3–4 fresh green chillies, such as
   jalapeño or serrano, deseeded
   and finely chopped
½–1 tsp ground cumin
3–4 spring onions (scallions), finely
   chopped
salt

1 To make the jalapeño salsa, put the onion in a bowl with the garlic, jalapeños, lemon juice and cumin. Season with salt and stir together. Cover and chill until required.

2 To make a chunky-textured salsa cruda, stir all the ingredients together in a bowl, adding salt to taste. Cover and chill until required.

3 To make a smoother-textured salsa, process the ingredients in a blender or food processor. Cover and chill until required.

VARIATION

For the salsa cruda, substitute finely chopped orange segments and deseeded diced cucumber for the tomatoes to add a fresh, fruity taste.

COOK'S TIP

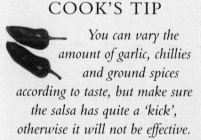

You can vary the amount of garlic, chillies and ground spices according to taste, but make sure the salsa has quite a 'kick', otherwise it will not be effective.

Chipotle Salsa

Chipotles are the smoked jalapeño chilli sold either dried or in cans, packed in a spicy flavourful marinade called adobo. Here the marinade from the canned version is used to perk up a simple fresh tomato salsa.

Makes about 450 ml/16 fl oz/2 cups

INGREDIENTS

450 g/1 lb ripe juicy tomatoes, diced
3–5 garlic cloves, finely chopped
½ bunch fresh coriander (cilantro) leaves, coarsely chopped
1 small onion, chopped

1–2 tsp adobo marinade from canned chipotle chillies
½–1 tsp sugar
lime juice, to taste
salt

pinch of cinnamon (optional)
pinch of ground allspice (optional)
pinch of ground cumin (optional)

1 Put the tomatoes, garlic and coriander (cilantro) in a blender or food processor.

2 Process the mixture until it is smooth, then add the onion, adobo marinade, sugar.

3 Squeeze in lime juice to taste. Season with salt to taste, then add the cinnamon, allspice or cumin, if wished.

4 Serve at once, or cover and chill until ready to serve, although the salsa is at its best when served freshly made.

COOK'S TIP

To simplify preparation, the fresh tomatoes can be replaced with a 400 g/14 oz can chopped tomatoes.

COOK'S TIP

Canned chipotle chillies are available from specialist Mexican stores.

Cooked Chipotle Salsa

This rich, tomato-red chipotle salsa is sweet and tangy, delicious with anything barbecued (grilled), or dabbed into a taco or burrito.

Makes about 450 ml/16 fl oz/2 cups

INGREDIENTS

3 dried chipotle chillies
1 onion, finely chopped
400 g/14 oz can tomatoes, including their juices
2–3 tbsp dark brown (molasses) sugar

2–3 garlic cloves, finely chopped
pinch of ground cinnamon
pinch of ground cloves or allspice
large pinch of ground cumin
juice of ½ lemon

1 tbsp extra-virgin olive oil
lemon rind strips, to garnish

1 Place the chillies in a pan with enough water to cover. Protecting your face against fumes and making sure the kitchen is well ventilated, bring the chillies and water to the boil. Cook for about 5 minutes, then remove from heat, cover and leave to stand until softened.

2 Remove the chillies from the water with a slotted spoon. Cut away and discard the stem and seeds, then either scrape the flesh from the skins or chop up the whole chillies.

3 Put the onion in a pan with the tomatoes and sugar and cook over a medium heat, stirring, until thickened.

4 Remove from the heat and add the garlic, cinnamon, cloves, cumin, lemon juice, olive oil and prepared chipotle chillies. Season with salt to taste and leave to cool. Serve garnished with lemon rind.

COOK'S TIP

Do not inhale the fumes given off during the boiling process as they can irritate your lungs.

COOK'S TIP

This salsa freezes extremely well. Freeze in an ice-cube tray, then pop the cubes out and store in a plastic bag, ready to use for individual portions.

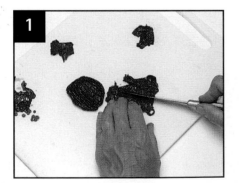

Hot Mexican Salsas

These salsas capture the inimitable tangy, spicy flavour of Mexico. Choose from a fresh minty fruit salsa, charred chilli salsa or a spicy 'green' salsa.

Serves 4–6

INGREDIENTS

TROPICAL FRUIT SALSA:

½ sweet ripe pineapple, peeled, cored and diced

1 mango or papaya, peeled, deseeded and diced

½–1 fresh green chilli, such as jalapeño or serrano, deseeded and chopped

½–1 fresh red chilli, chopped

½ red onion, chopped

1 tbsp sugar

juice of 1 lime

3 tbsp chopped fresh mint

salt

SCORCHED CHILLI SALSA:

1 green (bell) pepper

2–3 fresh green chillies, such as jalapeño or serrano

2 garlic cloves, finely chopped

juice of ½ lime

1 tsp salt

large pinch of dried oregano

large pinch of ground cumin

2–3 tbsp extra-virgin olive oil or vegetable oil

SALSA VERDE:

450 g/1 lb oz canned tomatillos, drained and chopped, or tart tomatoes, chopped

1–2 fresh green chillies, such as jalapeño or serrano, deseeded and finely chopped

1 green (bell) pepper or large mild green chilli, such as anaheim or poblano, deseeded and chopped

1 small onion, chopped

1 bunch fresh coriander (cilantro) leaves, finely chopped

½ tsp ground cumin

salt

1 To make the tropical fruit salsa, combine all the ingredients in a large bowl, adding salt to taste. Cover the bowl and chill in the refrigerator until required.

2 For scorched chilli salsa, char the chillies and (bell) pepper in an ungreased frying pan (skillet). Cool, deseed, skin and chop. Mix with the garlic, lime juice, salt and oil. Top with oregano and cumin.

3 For salsa verde, combine the ingredients in a bowl, adding salt to taste. If a smoother sauce is preferred, blend the ingredients in a food processor. Spoon into a bowl to serve.

Salsa of Marinated Chipotle Chillies

Dried chipotle chillies make a spicy-sweet smoky relish, good for adding to tostadas, tacos and any other tortilla dish.

Serves 4–6

INGREDIENTS

6 dried chipotle chillies
6 tbsp tomato ketchup (catsup)
350 g/12 oz ripe tomatoes, diced
1 large onion, chopped
5 garlic cloves, chopped
2 tbsp cider vinegar
300 ml/10 fl oz/1¼ cups water

1 tbsp extra-virgin olive oil
2 tbsp sugar, preferably molasses
  sugar
pinch of salt
¼ tsp ground allspice
¼ tsp ground cloves
¼ tsp ground cinnamon

¼ tsp ground cumin
3–4 tbsp lime juice or combination of
  pineapple and lemon juice
pepper

1 Place the chipotles in a pan with enough water to cover. Bring to the boil, taking care not to inhale the fumes given off as they can irritate your lungs. Simmer, covered, for about 20 minutes, then remove from the heat and leave to cool.

2 Remove the chillies from the water. Cut away and discard the stem and seeds, then either scrape the flesh from the skins or chop up the whole chillies.

3 Place the tomato ketchup (catsup) and tomatoes in a pan with the onion, chillies, garlic, vinegar, water, olive oil, sugar, salt, allspice, cloves, cinnamon and cumin. Bring to the boil. Reduce the heat and simmer for about 15 minutes until the mixture has thickened.

4 Season with salt and pepper to taste, then stir in the fruit juice and use as required.

Fresh Pineapple Salsa

This sweet fruity salsa is fresh and fragrant, a wonderful foil to spicy food from the barbecue (grill).

Serves 4

INGREDIENTS

½ ripe pineapple
juice of 1 lime or lemon
1 garlic clove, finely chopped
1 spring onion (scallion),
   thinly sliced

½–1 fresh green or red chilli,
   deseeded and finely chopped
½ red (bell) pepper, deseeded and
   chopped
3 tbsp chopped fresh mint

3 tbsp chopped fresh coriander
   (cilantro)
pinch of salt
pinch of sugar

1 Using a sharp knife, cut off the top and bottom of the pineapple. Place upright on a board, then slice off the skin, cutting downwards. Cut the flesh into slices, halve the slices and remove the cores, if wished. Dice the flesh. Reserve any juice that accumulates as you cut the pineapple.

2 Place the pineapple in a bowl and stir in the lime juice, garlic, spring onion (scallion), chopped chilli and red (bell) pepper.

3 Stir in the chopped fresh mint and coriander (cilantro). Add the salt and sugar and stir well to combine all the ingredients. Chill until ready to serve.

COOK'S TIP

A fresh pineapple is ripe if it has a sweet aroma. The flesh will still be fairly firm to touch. Still, fresh-looking leaves are a sign of good condition.

VARIATION

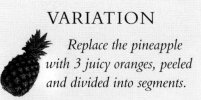
Replace the pineapple with 3 juicy oranges, peeled and divided into segments.

Crab & Avocado Soft Tacos

Crab meat and avocado make an elegant yet very authentic filling for tacos.
Eat one and you will be transported to a beach somewhere south of Acapulo!

Serves 4

INGREDIENTS

8 corn tortillas
1 avocado
lime or lemon juice, for tossing
4–6 tbsp soured cream
250–275 g/9–10 oz cooked
   crab meat

½ lime
½ fresh green chilli, such as jalapeño
   or serrano, deseeded and chopped
   or thinly sliced
1 ripe tomato, deseeded and diced
½ small onion, finely chopped

2 tbsp chopped fresh coriander
   (cilantro)
salsa of your choice, to serve
   (optional)

1 Heat the tortillas in an ungreased non-stick frying pan (skillet), sprinkling them with a few drops of water as they heat; wrap in a clean tea towel (dish cloth) as you work to keep them warm.

2 Cut the avocado in half around the stone (pit). Twist apart, then remove the stone (pit) with a knife. Carefully peel off the skin from the avocado, slice the flesh and toss in lime or lemon juice to prevent any discoloration.

3 Spread one tortilla with soured cream. Top with crab meat, a squeeze of lime and a sprinkling of chilli, tomato, onion, coriander (cilantro) and avocado, adding a splash of salsa if desired. Repeat the procedure with the remaining tortillas and serve immediately.

VARIATION

To transform into tostadas, fry the tortillas in a small amount of oil in a non-stick pan until crisp. Top one crisp tortilla with the filling, as in Step 3. Prepare a second tortilla with the filling and place on top of the first filled tortilla. Repeat once more, to make a small tower, top with shredded lettuce and serve.

Fish Tacos Ensenada Style

These tacos of fried fish chunks and red cabbage salad are served up in the cantinas and fondas of the coastal town of Ensenada, in Mexico's Baja California.

Serves 4

INGREDIENTS

about 450 g/1 lb firm-fleshed white
   fish, such as red snapper or cod
¼ tsp dried oregano
¼ tsp ground cumin
1 tsp mild chilli powder
2 garlic cloves, finely chopped

3 tbsp plain (all-purpose) flour
vegetable oil, for frying
¼ red cabbage, thinly sliced or
   shredded
juice of 2 limes
hot pepper sauce or salsa to taste

8 corn tortillas
1 tbsp chopped fresh coriander
   (cilantro)
½ onion, chopped (optional)
salt and pepper
salsa of your choice

1 Place the fish on a plate and sprinkle with half the oregano, cumin, chilli powder and garlic and salt and pepper, then dust with the flour.

2 Heat the oil in a frying pan (skillet) until it is smoking, then fry the fish in several batches until it is golden on the outside, and just tender in the middle. Remove from the pan and place on paper towels to drain.

3 Combine the cabbage with the remaining oregano, cumin, chilli and garlic, then stir in the lime juice, salt and hot pepper sauce to taste. Set aside.

4 Heat the tortillas in an ungreased non-stick frying pan (skillet), sprinkling with a few drops of water as they heat; wrap the tortillas in a clean tea towel (dish cloth) as you work to keep them warm. Alternatively, heat

through in a stack in the pan, alternating the tortillas from the top to the bottom so that they warm evenly.

5 Place some of the warm fried fish in each tortilla, along with a large spoonful of the hot cabbage salad. Sprinkle with chopped fresh coriander (cilantro) and onion, if desired. Add the salsa to taste and serve immediately.

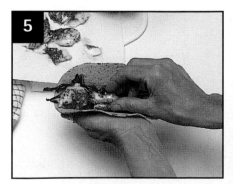

Fish & Refried Bean Tostadas with Green Salsa

Crisp tostadas are topped with spiced fish, refried beans and crunchy lettuce – perfect for a well-balanced lunch.

Serves 4

INGREDIENTS

about 450 g/1 lb firm-fleshed white
   fish, such as red snapper or cod
120 ml/4 fl oz/½ cup fish stock, or
   water mixed with a fish stock cube
¼ tsp ground cumin
¼ tsp mild chilli powder
pinch of dried oregano
4 garlic cloves, finely chopped

juice of ½ lemon or lime
8 soft corn tortillas
vegetable oil, for frying
400 g/14 oz can refried beans,
   warmed with 2 tbsp water to thin
salsa of your choice
2–3 leaves cos (romaine) lettuce,
   shredded

3 tbsp chopped fresh coriander
   (cilantro)
2 tbsp chopped onion
salt and pepper

TO GARNISH:
soured cream
chopped fresh herbs

1 Put the fish in a pan with the fish stock, cumin, chilli, oregano, garlic and salt and pepper. Gently bring to the boil, then immediately remove from the heat and leave the fish to cool in the cooking liquid.

2 When cool enough to handle, remove from the liquid with a slotted spoon; reserve the cooking liquid. Break the fish up into bite-sized pieces, put in a bowl, sprinkle with the lemon or lime juice and set aside.

3 To make tostadas, fry the tortillas in a small amount of oil in a non-stick frying pan (skillet) until crisp. Spread the tostadas evenly with the warm refried beans.

4 Gently reheat the fish with a little of the reserved cooking liquid, then spoon the fish on top of the beans. Top each tostada with some of the salsa, lettuce, chopped fresh coriander (cilantro) and onion. Garnish each one with a dollop of soured cream and a sprinkling of chopped fresh herbs. Serve immediately.

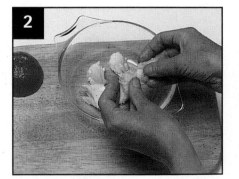

Fish Burritos

You can use any seafood you like in this tasty Mexican snack.
Tacos are eaten in the hand, like sandwiches.

Serves 4–6

INGREDIENTS

about 450 g/1 lb firm-fleshed white
   fish, such as red snapper or cod
¼ tsp ground cumin
pinch of dried oregano
4 garlic finely cloves, chopped

120 ml/4 fl oz fish stock, or water
   mixed with a fish stock cube
juice of ½ lemon or lime
8 flour tortillas
2 ripe tomatoes, diced

1 quantity Salsa Cruda (see page 96)
2–3 leaves cos (romaine) lettuce,
   shredded
salt and pepper
lemon slices, to serve

1 Season the fish with salt and pepper, then put in a pan with the cumin, oregano, garlic and enough fish stock to cover.

2 Bring to the boil, then cook for about a minute. Remove the pan from the heat and leave the fish to cool in the cooking liquid for about 30 minutes.

3 Remove the fish from the stock and break up into bite-sized pieces. Sprinkle with the lemon or lime juice and set aside.

4 Heat the tortillas in an ungreased non-stick frying pan (skillet), sprinkling them with a few drops of water as they heat; wrap in a clean tea towel (dish cloth) as you work to keep them warm.

5 Arrange shredded lettuce in the middle of one tortilla, spoon on a few big chunks of the fish, then sprinkle with the tomato. Add salsa cruda. Repeat with the other tortillas and serve at once with lemon slices.

VARIATION

Cook several peeled waxy potatoes in the fish stock, then dice and serve wrapped up in the warm tortillas along with the lettuce, fish, tomato and salsa. Or add sliced lime-dressed avocado with the filling.

Chicken Tacos from Puebla

Seasoned chicken fills these soft tacos, along with creamy refried beans, avocado, smoky chipotle and soured cream. A feast of tastes!

Serves 4

INGREDIENTS

8 corn tortillas

2 tsp vegetable oil

225–350 g/8–12 oz leftover cooked chicken, diced or shredded

225 g/8 oz can refried beans, warmed with a 2 tbsp water to thin

¼ tsp ground cumin

¼ tsp dried oregano

1 avocado, stoned (pitted), sliced and tossed with lime juice

Salsa Verde (see page 102) or salsa of your choice

1 canned chipotle chilli in adobo marinade, chopped, or bottled chipotle salsa

175 ml/6 fl oz/¾ cup soured cream

½ onion, chopped

handful of lettuce leaves

5 radishes, diced

salt and pepper

---

1 Heat the tortillas in an ungreased non-stick frying pan (skillet) in a stack, alternating the top and bottom tortillas so that the tortillas heat evenly. Wrap in kitchen foil or a clean tea towel (dish cloth) to keep warm.

2 Heat the oil in a frying pan (skillet), add the chicken and heat through. Season with salt and pepper to taste.

3 Combine the refried beans with the cumin and oregano.

4 Spread one tortilla with warm refried beans, then top with a spoonful of the chicken, a slice or two of avocado, a dab of salsa, chipotle to taste, a dollop of soured cream and a sprinkling of onion, lettuce and radishes. Season with salt and pepper to taste, then roll up, as tightly as you can.

Repeat with the remaining tortillas and serve at once.

VARIATION

Replace the chicken with 450 g/1 lb minced (ground) beef browned with a seasoning of chopped onion, mild chilli powder and ground cumin to taste.

Chile Verde Tacos with Pinto Beans

This is also an ideal way of using up any leftover spicy stewed meat – use in place of the Chile Verde and you have an almost instant meal!

Serves 4

INGREDIENTS

8 corn tortillas
vegetable oil, for greasing
400 g/14 oz can pinto beans
⅓ quantity Chile Verde
  (see page 204)
3 ripe tomatoes, diced
½ onion, chopped

2 tbsp finely chopped fresh
  coriander (cilantro)

TO GARNISH:
soured cream
mild chilli powder

TO SERVE:
salsa of your choice
shredded lettuce

1 Heat the tortillas in a lightly greased non-stick frying pan (skillet); wrap the tortillas in a tea towel (dish cloth) as you work to keep them warm.

2 Drain the beans, reserving a few tablespoons of the liquid. Heat the beans in a pan with the reserved canned liquid.

3 Heat through the Chile Verde in a pan until just boiling.

4 Spoon some of the drained beans on to a warm tortilla. Top with warm Chile Verde, then sprinkle with tomatoes, onion and fresh coriander (cilantro). Roll up and repeat with the remaining tortillas. Garnish with a spoonful of soured cream and a sprinkling of chilli powder, then serve at once with salsa and shredded lettuce.

VARIATION

For a tostada version, heat tostadas (crisp tortillas) under the grill (broiler), then spread with warmed slightly thinned refried beans and top with the Chile Verde, shredded lettuce, a little grated pecorino cheese, salsa, onion, fresh coriander (cilantro) and soured cream. Serve at once.

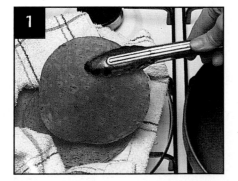

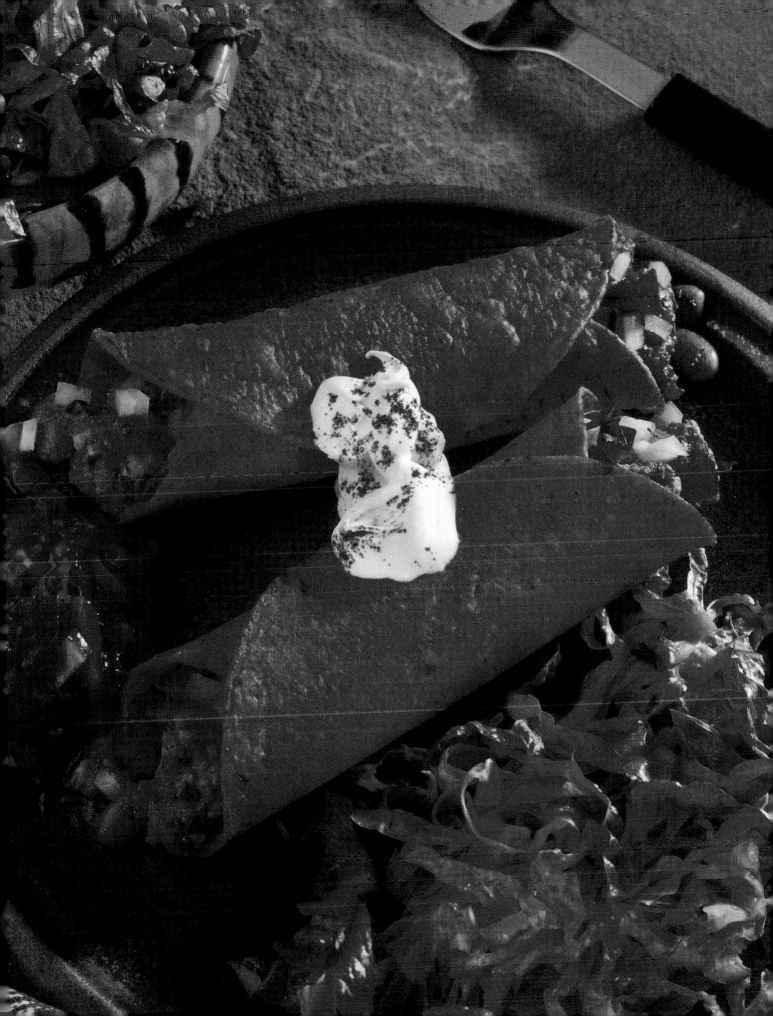

Chicken Tostadas with Green Salsa & Chipotle

Chicken makes a delicate yet satisfying topping for crisp tostadas. You do not need to prepare chicken especially for this recipe: any leftover chicken is equally delicious.

Serves 4–6

INGREDIENTS

6 corn tortillas
vegetable oil, for frying
450 g/1 lb skinned boned chicken breast or thigh, cut into strips or small pieces
225 ml/8 fl oz/1 cup chicken stock
2 garlic cloves, finely chopped
400 g/14 oz refried beans (see page 144) or canned

large pinch of ground cumin
225 g/8 oz grated cheese
1 tbsp chopped fresh coriander (cilantro)
2 ripe tomatoes, diced
handful of crisp lettuce leaves, such as cos (romaine) or iceberg, shredded
4–6 radishes, diced

3 spring onions (scallions), thinly sliced
1 ripe avocado, stoned (pitted), diced or sliced and tossed with lime juice
soured cream to taste
1–2 canned chipotle chillies in adobo marinade, or dried chipotle reconstituted (see page 100), cut into thin strips

1 To make tostadas, fry the tortillas in a small amount of oil in a non-stick pan until crisp.

2 Put the chicken in a pan with the stock and garlic. Bring to the boil, then reduce the heat and cook for 1–2 minutes until the chicken begins to turn opaque.

3 Remove the chicken from the heat and leave to steep in its hot liquid to cook through.

4 Heat the beans with enough water to form a smooth purée. Add the cumin and keep warm.

5 Reheat the tostadas under a preheated grill (broiler), if necessary. Spread the hot beans on the tostadas, then sprinkle with the grated cheese. Lift the cooked chicken from the liquid and divide between the tostadas. Top with the coriander (cilantro), tomatoes, lettuce, radishes, spring onions (scallions), avocado, soured cream and a few strips of chipotle. Serve immediately.

Vegetable Tostadas

*Top a crisp tostada (fried tortilla) with spicy vegetables
and you have a vegetarian feast!*

Serves 4

INGREDIENTS

4 corn tortillas
vegetable oil, for frying
2–3 tbsp extra-virgin olive oil or
  vegetable oil
2 potatoes, diced
1 carrot, diced
3 garlic cloves, finely chopped
1 red (bell) pepper, deseeded and
  diced

1 tsp mild chilli powder
1 tsp paprika
½ tsp ground cumin
3–4 ripe tomatoes, diced
115 g/4 oz green beans, blanched and
  cut into bite-sized lengths
several large pinches dried oregano
400 g/14 oz cooked black beans,
  drained

225 g/8 oz crumbled feta cheese
3–4 leaves cos (romaine) lettuce,
  shredded
3–4 spring onions (scallions), thinly
  sliced

1 To make tostadas, fry the tortillas in a small amount of oil in a non-stick pan until crisp.

2 Heat the olive oil in a frying pan (skillet), add the potatoes and carrot and cook until softened. Add the garlic, red (bell) pepper, chilli powder, paprika and cumin. Cook for 2–3 minutes until the peppers have softened.

3 Add the tomatoes, green beans and oregano. Cook for 8–10 minutes until the vegetables are tender and form a sauce-like mixture. The mixture should not be too dry; add a little water if necessary, to keep it moist.

4 Heat the black beans in a pan with a tiny amount of water, and keep warm. Reheat the tostadas under the grill (broiler).

5 Layer the beans over the hot tostadas, then sprinkle with the cheese and top with a few spoonfuls of the hot vegetables in sauce. Serve at once, each tostada sprinkled with the lettuce and spring onions (scallions).

Broccoli Enchiladas in Mild Chilli Salsa

This is reminiscent of a sort of Mexican spiced cannelloni, with flour tortillas taking the place of the pasta tubes.

Serves 4

INGREDIENTS

450 g/1 lb broccoli florets
225 g/8 oz ricotta cheese
1 garlic clove, chopped
½ tsp ground cumin
175–200 g/6–8 oz Cheddar cheese, grated
6–8 tbsp freshly grated Parmesan cheese

1 egg, lightly beaten
4–6 flour tortillas
vegetable oil, for greasing
1 quantity Mild Red Chilli Sauce (see page 86)
225 ml/8 fl oz/1 cup chicken or vegetable stock
½ onion, finely chopped

3–4 tbsp chopped fresh coriander (cilantro)
3 ripe tomatoes, diced
salt and pepper
hot salsa, to serve

1 Bring a pan of salted water to the boil, add the broccoli, bring back to the boil and blanch for 1 minute. Drain, refresh under cold running water, then drain again. Cut off the stems, peel and chop. Dice the heads.

2 Mix the broccoli with the ricotta cheese, garlic, cumin, half the Cheddar and Parmesan in a bowl. Mix in the egg and season with salt and pepper.

3 Heat the tortillas in a lightly greased non-stick frying pan (skillet); then wrap in kitchen foil. Fill the tortillas with the broccoli mixture, rolling them up.

4 Arrange the tortilla rolls in an ovenproof dish, then pour the mild chilli sauce over the top. Pour over the stock.

5 Top with the remaining Cheddar and Parmesan cheeses and bake in a preheated oven at 190°C/375°F/Gas Mark 5 for about 30 minutes. Serve sprinkled with the onion, fresh coriander (cilantro) and tomatoes. Serve with a hot salsa.

Cheese Enchiladas with Mole Flavours

Mole sauce makes a delicious enchilada – a good reason to make yourself a big pot of Mole Poblano (see page 90). But if you are short of time, you can always use bottled mole paste instead.

Serves 4–6

INGREDIENTS

8 corn tortillas
vegetable oil, for greasing
450 ml/16 fl oz/2 cups mole sauce
about 225 g/8 oz grated cheese, such
   as Cheddar, mozzarella, asiago or
   Mexican queso oaxaco, one type or
   a mixture

225 ml/8 fl oz/1 cup chicken or
   vegetable stock
5 spring onions (scallions), thinly
   sliced
2–3 tbsp chopped fresh coriander
   (cilantro)

handful of cos (romaine) lettuce
   leaves, shredded
1 avocado, stoned (pitted), diced and
   tossed in lime juice
4 tbsp soured cream
salsa of your choice

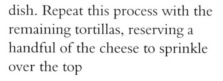

1 Heat the tortillas in a lightly greased non-stick frying pan (skillet); wrap the tortillas in kitchen foil as you work to keep them warm.

2 Dip the tortillas into the mole sauce, and pile up on a plate. Fill the inside of the top sauced tortilla with a few spoonfuls of cheese. Roll up and arrange in a shallow ovenproof dish. Repeat this process with the remaining tortillas, reserving a handful of the cheese to sprinkle over the top

3 Pour the rest of the mole sauce over the rolled tortillas, then pour the stock over the top. Sprinkle with the reserved cheese and cover with kitchen foil.

4 Bake in a preheated oven at 190°C/375°F/Gas Mark 5 until the tortillas are piping hot and the cheese filling melts.

5 Arrange the spring onions (scallions), fresh coriander (cilantro), lettuce, avocado and soured cream on top. Add salsa to taste. Serve at once.

Santa Fe
Red Chilli Enchiladas

These enchiladas are served stacked, in the traditional New Mexican style,
but you can always roll them up with the filling if you prefer.

Serves 4

INGREDIENTS

2-3 tbsp masa harina or 1 corn
   tortilla, crushed or crumbled
4 tbsp mild chilli powder, such as
   New Mexico
2 tbsp paprika
2 garlic cloves, finely chopped
¼ tsp ground cumin
pinch of ground cinnamon

pinch of ground allspice
pinch of dried oregano
1 tbsp lime juice
1 litre/1¾ pints/4 cups vegetable,
   chicken or beef stock, simmering
8 flour tortillas
about 450 g/1 lb cooked chicken or
   pork, cut into pieces
80 g/3 oz grated cheese

1 tbsp extra-virgin olive oil
4-6 eggs

TO SERVE:
½ onion, finely chopped
1 tbsp finely chopped fresh coriander
   (cilantro)
salsa of your choice

1 Mix the masa harina with the chilli powder, paprika, garlic, cumin, cinnamon, allspice, oregano and enough water to make a thin paste. Process in a blender or food processor until smooth.

2 Stir the paste into the simmering stock, reduce the heat and cook until it thickens slightly, then remove the sauce from the heat and stir in the lime juice.

3 Dip the tortillas into the warm sauce. Cover one tortilla with some of the cooked meat. Top with a second dipped tortilla and more meat filling.

Make 3 more towers in this way, then transfer to an ovenproof dish.

4 Pour the remaining sauce over the tortillas, then sprinkle with the grated cheese. Bake in a preheated oven at 180°C/ 350°F/ Gas Mark 4 for 15-20 minutes or until the cheese has melted.

5 Meanwhile, heat the olive oil in a non-stick frying pan (skillet) and cook the eggs until the whites are set and the yolks are still soft.

6 To serve the enchiladas, top each with a fried egg. Serve with the onion mixed with fresh coriander (cilantro) and salsa.

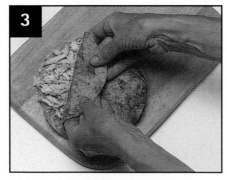

Chicken Tortilla Flutes with Guacamole

These crisply fried, rolled tortillas are known as flauta, *meaning 'flutes' in Mexican, because of their delicate, long shape.*

Serves 4

INGREDIENTS

8 corn tortillas
350 g/12 oz cooked chicken, diced
1 tsp mild chilli powder
1 onion, chopped

1–2 tbsp crème fraîche
vegetable oil, for frying
2 tbsp finely chopped fresh coriander
   (cilantro)

1 quantity of Guacamole
   (see page 28)
salsa of your choice
salt

1 Heat the tortillas in an ungreased non-stick frying pan (skillet) in a stack, alternating the top and bottom tortillas so that all of the tortillas warm evenly. Wrap in kitchen foil or a clean tea towel (dish cloth) to keep warm

2 Place the chicken in a bowl with the chilli powder, half the onion, half the coriander (cilantro) and salt to taste. Add enough crème fraîche to hold the mixture together.

3 Arrange 2 corn tortillas on the work surface so that they are overlapping, then spoon some of the filling along the centre. Roll up very tightly and secure in place with a toothpick or two. Repeat with the remaining tortillas and filling.

4 Heat oil in a deep frying pan (skillet) until hot and fry the rolls until golden and crisp. Carefully remove from the oil and drain on paper towels.

5 Serve immediately, garnishing with the guacamole, salsa, diced tomato and the remaining onion and fresh coriander (cilantro).

VARIATION

Replace the chicken with seafood, such as cooked prawns (shrimp) or crab meat, and serve the rolls with lemon wedges.

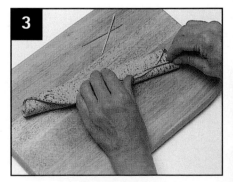

Pork Quesadilla with Pinto Beans

These melt-in-the-mouth tortilla parcels have a lovely pork, bean and melted cheese filling. Any leftover cooked meat may be used instead of the Carnitas.

Serves 4

INGREDIENTS

1 quantity of Carnitas (see page 208) or about 100 g/3½ oz cooked pork strips per person
1 ripe tomato, deseeded and diced
½ onion, chopped
3 tbsp chopped fresh coriander (cilantro)
4 large flour tortillas

350 g/12 oz grated or thinly sliced cheese, such as mozzarella or gouda
about 375 g/13½ oz cooked drained pinto beans
hot salsa of your choice or bottled hot sauce, to taste

pickled jalapeño chillies, cut into thin rings, to taste
vegetable oil, for frying

TO SERVE:
pickled chillies
mixed salad

1 Heat the Carnitas in a pan and keep hot over a low heat.

2 Combine the tomato, onion and coriander (cilantro) in a bowl and set aside.

3 Heat a tortilla in an ungreased non-stick frying pan (skillet). Sprinkle the tortilla with cheese, then top with some of the meat, beans and reserved tomato mixture. Add salsa and pickled jalapeños to taste. Fold over the sides to make a parcel.

4 Heat the parcels gently on each side in the frying pan (skillet), adding a few drops of oil to keep it all supple and succulent, until the tortilla is golden and the cheese inside has melted. Keep warm. Repeat with the remaining tortillas and filling.

5 Transfer the quesadillas to a plate and serve at once, with pickled chillies and salad.

Casserole of Tortilla Chips & Chorizo

Called chilaquiles *in Mexican, this dish turns everyday leftovers into something quite special! Excellent served for brunch, topped with an egg.*

Serves 6–8

INGREDIENTS

12 stale tortillas, cut into strips
1 tbsp vegetable oil
2–3 chorizo sausages, thinly sliced or
  diced
2 garlic cloves, finely chopped

225 g/8 oz chopped canned tomatoes
3 tbsp chopped fresh coriander
  (cilantro)
450 ml/16 fl oz/2 cups chicken or
  vegetable stock

225 g/8 oz grated cheese
1 onion, finely chopped
salt and pepper

1 Place the tortilla strips in a roasting tin (pan), toss with the oil and bake in a preheated oven at 190°C/375°F/Gas Mark 5 for about 30 minutes until they are crisp and golden.

2 Brown the chorizo with the garlic in a frying pan (skillet) until the meat is cooked; pour away any excess fat. Add the tomatoes and the coriander (cilantro) and season with salt and pepper to taste. Set aside.

3 In an ovenproof dish, about 30 cm/12 inches square, layer the tortilla chips and chorizo mixture, finishing with the tortilla chips.

4 Pour the stock over the top of the dish, then sprinkle with the cheese. Bake in a preheated oven at 190°C/375°F/Gas Mark 5 for about 40 minutes until the tortilla chips are fairly soft.

5 Serve immediately, sprinkled with the chopped onion.

VARIATION

Serve with a fried egg or two alongside. The soft yolk tastes wonderful with the spicy casserole – offer a bowl of spicy salsa for those who want it hotter.

Green Chilli & Chicken Chilaquiles

Easy to put together, this dish makes a perfect mid-week supper.
Use tortilla chips instead of baking the tortillas, if you prefer.

Serves 4–6

INGREDIENTS

12 stale tortillas, cut into strips

1 tbsp vegetable oil

1 small cooked chicken, meat
   removed from the bones and cut
   into bite-sized pieces

Salsa Verde (see page 102)

3 tbsp chopped fresh coriander
   (cilantro)

1 tsp finely chopped fresh oregano
   or thyme

4 garlic cloves, finely chopped

¼ tsp ground cumin

350 g/12 oz grated cheese, such
   as Cheddar, manchego or
   mozzarella

450 ml/16 fl oz/2 cups chicken
   stock

about 115 g/4 oz/1⅓ cups freshly
   grated Parmesan cheese

TO SERVE:

350 ml/12 fl oz/1½ cups crème
   fraîche or soured cream

3–5 spring onions (scallions), thinly
   sliced

pickled chillies

1 Place the tortilla strips in a roasting tin (pan), toss with the oil and bake in a preheated oven at 190°C/375°F/Gas Mark 5 for about 30 minutes until they are crisp and golden.

2 Arrange the chicken in a 23 x 33 cm/9 x 13 inch casserole, then sprinkle with half the salsa, coriander (cilantro), oregano, garlic, cumin and some of the soft

cheese. Repeat these layers and top with the tortilla strips.

3 Pour the stock over the top, then sprinkle with the remaining cheeses.

4 Bake in a preheated oven at 190°C/375°F/Gas Mark 5 for about 30 minutes until heated through and the cheese is lightly golden in areas.

5 Serve garnished with the crème fraîche, sliced spring onions (scallions) and pickled chillies to taste.

VARIATION

For a vegetarian Mexicana filling, add diced sautéed tofu and sweetcorn kernels in place of the cooked chicken.

Tamales

Traditional Mexican fare, tamales are large dumplings of corn flour, stuffed with a moist filling, then wrapped in either banana leaves or husks of corn. They make attractive party food.

Serves 4–6

INGREDIENTS

6 tbsp lard or vegetable shortening
½ tsp salt
pinch of sugar
pinch of ground cumin
225 g/8 oz masa harina
½ tsp baking powder
about 225 ml/8 fl oz/1 cup beef,
   chicken or vegetable stock

8–10 corn husks or several banana
   leaves, cut into 30 cm/12 inch
   squares

TO SERVE:
shredded lettuce
salsa of your choice

FILLING:
115 g/4 oz cooked sweetcorn, mixed
   with a little grated cheese and
   chopped green chilli, or simmered
   pork in a mild chilli sauce

1 If using corn husks, soak in hot water to cover for at least 3 hours or overnight. If using banana leaves, warm them by placing over an open flame for just a few seconds, to make them pliable.

2 To make the tamale dough, beat the lard or shortening until fluffy, then beat in the salt, sugar, cumin, masa harina and baking powder until the mixture resembles tiny crumbs.

3 Add the stock very gradually, in several batches, beating until mixture becomes fluffy and resembles whipped cream

4 Spread 1–2 tablespoons of the tamale mixture on either a soaked and drained corn husk or a piece of pliable heated banana leaf.

5 Spoon in the filling. Fold the sides of the husks or leaves over the filling to enclose. Wrap each parcel in a square of kitchen foil, and arrange in a steamer.

6 Pour hot water in the bottom of the steamer, cover, and boil. Cook for 40–60 minutes, topping up the water in the bottom of the steamer when needed. Remove the tamales and serve.

Burritos of Lamb & Black Beans

Stir-fried marinated lamb strips are paired with earthy black beans in these tasty burritos.

Serves 4

INGREDIENTS

650 g/1 lb 5 oz lean lamb
3 garlic cloves, finely chopped
juice of ½ lime
½ tsp mild chilli powder
½ tsp ground cumin

large pinch of dried oregano leaves, crushed
1–2 tbsp extra-virgin olive oil
400 g/14 oz cooked black beans, seasoned with a little cumin, salt and pepper

4 large flour tortillas
2–3 tbsp chopped fresh coriander (cilantro)
salsa, preferably Chipotle Salsa (see page 98)
salt and pepper

1 Slice the lamb into thin strips, then combine with the garlic, lime juice, chilli powder, cumin, oregano and olive oil. Season with salt and pepper. Leave to marinate in the refrigerator for 4 hours.

2 Warm the black beans with a little water in a pan.

3 Heat the tortillas in an ungreased non-stick frying pan (skillet), sprinkling them with a few drops of water as they heat; wrap the tortillas in a clean tea towel (dish cloth) as you work to keep them warm. Alternatively, heat through in a stack in the pan, alternating the top and bottom tortillas so that they warm evenly. Wrap to keep warm.

4 Stir-fry the lamb in a heavy-based non-stick frying pan over high heat until browned on all sides. Remove from the heat.

5 Spoon some of the beans and browned meat into a tortilla, sprinkle with coriander (cilantro), then dab with salsa and roll up. Repeat with the remaining tortillas and serve at once.

VARIATION

Add a spoonful or two of cooked rice to each burrito.

Mexican Beans

A pot of beans, bubbling away on the stove, is the basic everyday food of Mexico – delicious and healthy!

Serves 4–6

INGREDIENTS

500 g/1 lb 2 oz dried pinto or borlotti
  beans
sprig of fresh mint
sprig of fresh thyme
sprig of fresh flat-leaf parsley

1 onion, cut into chunks
salt

TO SERVE:
shreds of spring onion (scallion)
warmed flour or corn tortillas

1 Pick through the beans and remove any bits of grit or stone. Cover the beans with cold water and leave to soak overnight. If you want to cut down on soaking time, bring the beans to the boil, cook for 5 minutes, then remove from the heat and leave to stand, covered, for 2 hours.

2 Drain the beans, place in a pan and cover with fresh water and the mint, thyme and parsley. Bring to the boil, then reduce the heat to very low and cook gently, covered, for about 2 hours until the beans are tender. The best way to check that they are done is to sample a bean or two every so often, after 1¾ hours cooking time.

3 Add the onion and continue to cook until the onion and beans are very tender.

4 To serve as a side dish, drain, season with salt and serve in a bowl lined with warmed corn or flour tortillas, garnished with spring onion (scallion) shreds (see Cook's Tip).

COOK'S TIP

If using the beans for Refried Beans (see page 144), do not drain as the liquid is required for the recipe.

COOK'S TIP

The length of time the beans take to cook will depend on the age of the beans – old beans take longer than younger beans; the mineral content of the water matters, too.

Refried Beans

One of Mexico's most famous dishes, refried beans, or frijoles refritos, *is incredibly versatile. Serve them piled on to crisp tostadas or crusty rolls, spooned beside rice or rolled into a tortilla.*

Serves 4–6

INGREDIENTS

1 quantity Mexican Beans, with their cooking liquid (see page 142)
1–2 onions, chopped

120 ml/4 fl oz/½ cup vegetable oil or 125 g/4½ oz lard or dripping
½ tsp ground cumin

salt
250 g/9 oz grated Cheddar cheese (optional)

1 Put two-thirds of the cooked beans, with their cooking liquid, in a food processor and process to a purée. Stir in the remaining whole beans. Set aside.

2 Heat the oil or fat in a heavy-based frying pan (skillet). Add the onions and cook until they are very soft. Sprinkle with cumin and salt to taste.

3 Ladle in a cupful of the bean mixture, and cook, stirring, until the beans reduce down to a thick mixture; the beans will darken slightly as they cook.

4 Continue adding the bean mixture, a ladleful at a time, stirring and reducing down the liquid before adding the next ladleful. You should end up with a thick, chunky purée.

5 If using cheese, sprinkle it over the beans and cover tightly until the heat in the pan melts the cheese. Alternatively, place under a preheated grill (broiler) to melt the cheese. Serve immediately.

VARIATION

Add several browned, broken-up chorizo sausages to the beans, along with a small tin of sardines, mashed to a paste. Serve stuffed into crusty rolls for a classic mollete, or as a party dip. Good spread on to crisp tostadas for an afternoon pick-me-up.

Mexican Refried Beans 'With Everything'

These are refried beans fit for a fiesta, rich with everything – bacon, fried onions, tomatoes, even a bit of beer! As delicious as it sounds!

Serves 4

INGREDIENTS

1–2 tbsp vegetable oil

1–1½ large onions, chopped

125 g/4½ oz bacon lardons or bacon cut into small pieces

3–4 garlic cloves, finely chopped

about 1 tsp ground cumin

½ tsp mild chilli powder

400 g/14 oz can tomatoes, diced and drained, reserving about 150–175 ml/5–6 fl oz/¾–¾ cup of their juices

400 g/14 oz can refried beans, broken up into pieces

100 ml/3½ fl oz/scant ½ cup beer

400 g/14 oz can pinto beans, drained

salt and pepper

TO SERVE:

warmed flour tortillas

soured cream

sliced pickled chillies

1 Heat the oil in a frying pan (skillet). Add the onion and bacon and fry for about 5 minutes until they are just turning brown. Stir in the garlic, cumin and chilli powder and continue to cook for a minute. Add the tomatoes and cook over a medium-high heat until the liquid has evaporated.

2 Add the refried beans and mash lightly in the pan with the tomato mixture, adding beer as needed to thin out the beans and make them smoother. Lower the heat and cook, stirring, until the mixture is smooth and creamy.

3 Add the pinto beans and stir well to combine; if the mixture is too thick, add a little of the reserved tomato juice. Adjust the spicing to taste. Season with salt and pepper and serve with warmed tortillas, soured cream and sliced chillies.

VARIATION

Top the dish with grated cheese, then pop under a preheated grill (broiler) to melt and sizzle. Serve at once. This makes a luscious filling for warm flour tortillas.

Spicy Fragrant Black Bean Chilli

Black beans are fragrant and flavourful; enjoy this chillied bean stew Mexican style with soft tortillas, or Californian style in a bowl with crisp tortillas chips crumbled in.

Serves 4

INGREDIENTS

400 g/14 oz dried black beans
2 tbsp olive oil
1 onion, chopped
5 garlic cloves, coarsely chopped
2 slices bacon, diced (optional)

½–1 tsp ground cumin
½–1 tsp mild red chilli powder
1 red (bell) pepper, diced
1 carrot, diced
400 g/14 oz fresh tomatoes, diced, or

chopped canned
1 bunch fresh coriander (cilantro), coarsely chopped
salt and pepper

1 Soak the beans overnight, then drain. Put in a pan, cover with water and bring to the boil. Boil for 10 minutes, then reduce the heat and simmer for about 1½ hours until tender. Drain well, reserving 225 ml/8 fl oz/1 cup of the cooking liquid.

2 Heat the oil in a frying pan (skillet). Add the onion and garlic and fry for 2 minutes, stirring. Stir in the bacon, if using, and cook, stirring occasionally,

until the bacon is cooked and the onion is soften.

3 Stir in the cumin and red chilli powder and continue to cook for a moment or two. Add the red (bell) pepper, carrot and tomatoes. Cook over a medium heat for about 5 minutes.

4 Add half the coriander (cilantro) and the beans and their reserved liquid. Season with salt and pepper. Simmer for 30–45

minutes or until very flavourful and thickened.

5 Stir through the remaining coriander (cilantro), adjust the seasoning and serve at once.

COOK'S TIP

You can use canned beans, if wished: drain and use 225 ml/ 8 fl oz/1 cup water for the liquid added in Step 4.

Rice with Lime

The tangy citrus taste of lime is marvellous with all sorts of rice dishes. Although not typically Mexican, you could add wild rice to this dish, if liked.

Serves 4

INGREDIENTS

2 tbsp vegetable oil
1 small onion, finely
   chopped
3 garlic cloves, finely chopped

175 g/6 oz long-grain rice
450 ml/16 fl oz/2 cups chicken or
   vegetable stock

juice of 1 lime
1 tbsp chopped fresh coriander
   (cilantro)

1 Heat the oil in a heavy-based pan or flameproof casserole. Add the onion and garlic and cook gently, stirring occasionally, for 2 minutes. Add the rice and cook for a further minute, stirring. Pour in the stock, increase the heat and bring the rice to the boil. Reduce the heat to a very low simmer.

2 Cover and cook the rice for about 10 minutes or until the rice is just tender and the liquid is absorbed.

3 Sprinkle in the lime juice and fork the rice to fluff up and to mix the juice in. Sprinkle with the coriander (cilantro) and serve.

COOK'S TIP

Garnish the rice with sautéed plantains: slice a ripe peeled plantain, preferably on the diagonal, then fry in a heavy-based pan in a small amount of oil until they have browned in spots and are tender. Arrange in the bowl of rice.

VARIATION

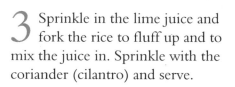

Fork about 225 g/8 oz cooked sweetcorn into the rice when it is almost but not quite cooked, then allow the sweetcorn to warm through as the rice finishes cooking. Sprinkle with diced cucumber and a squeeze of lime juice to add a fresh tang.

Cumin Rice
with Sweet (Bell) Peppers

Cumin seeds add a distinctive flavour to this colourful rice dish.
Serve as a side dish for any roasted or barbecued (grilled) meat.

Serves 4

INGREDIENTS

2 tbsp butter

1 tbsp vegetable oil

1 green (bell) pepper, deseeded
  and sliced

1 red (bell) pepper, deseeded
  and sliced

3 spring onions (scallions),
  thinly sliced

3–4 garlic cloves, finely chopped

175 g/6 oz/scant 1 cup long-grain
  rice

1½ tsp cumin seeds

½ tsp dried oregano or marjoram,
  crushed

450 ml/16 fl oz/2 cups chicken or
  vegetable stock

1 Heat the butter and oil in a heavy-based pan or flameproof casserole. Add the (bell) peppers and cook until softened.

2 Add the spring onions (scallions), garlic, rice and cumin seeds. Cook for about 5 minutes or until the rice turns slightly golden.

3 Add the oregano and stock to the pan or casserole, bring to the boil, then reduce the heat and cook for about 5 minutes.

4 Cover with a clean tea towel (dish cloth) and remove from the heat. Leave to steam for about 10 minutes, depending upon the age and maturity of the rice. If the rice is pretty mature, extend the initial cooking time to 10 minutes.

5 Fluff up the rice with a fork and serve at once.

VARIATION

Serve folded through a portion or two of black beans, and serve as a side dish with hearty roasted meat or poultry.

Green Rice

A paste of roasted onions, garlic and chillies, puréed with lots of green coriander (cilantro) leaves gives this rice a lovely fresh colour and stunning taste.

Serves 4

INGREDIENTS

1–2 onions, halved and unpeeled
6–8 large garlic cloves, unpeeled
1 large mild chilli, or 1 green (bell) pepper and 1 small green chilli
1 bunch fresh coriander (cilantro) leaves, chopped

225 ml/8 fl oz/1 cup chicken or vegetable stock
175 g/6 oz/scant 1 cup long-grain rice
80 ml/3 fl oz/⅓ cup vegetable or olive oil

salt and pepper
fresh coriander sprig, to garnish

1 Heat a heavy-based ungreased frying pan (skillet) and cook the onion, garlic, chilli and (bell) pepper, if using, until lightly charred on all sides, including the cut sides of the onions. Cover and leave to cool.

2 When cool enough to handle, remove the seeds and skin from the chilli and (bell) pepper, if using. Chop the flesh.

3 Remove the skins from the cooled onion and garlic and chop finely.

4 Place the vegetables in a food processor with the coriander (cilantro) leaves and stock, then process to a smooth thin purée.

5 Heat the oil in a heavy-based pan and fry the rice until it is glistening and lightly browned in places, stirring to prevent it from burning. Add the purée, cover and cook over a medium-low heat for 10–15 minutes until the rice is just tender.

6 Fluff up the rice with a fork, then cover and stand for

about 5 minutes. Adjust the seasoning, garnish with a sprig of coriander (cilantro) and serve.

COOK'S TIP

Leftover green rice is delicious mixed with minced (ground) beef and/or pork for savoury meatballs, or as a filling for (bell) peppers.

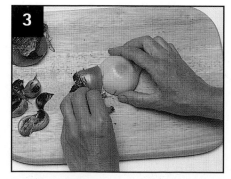

Rice with Black Beans

Any kind of bean cooking liquid is delicious for cooking rice
– black beans are particularly good for their startling grey colour and earthy flavour.

Serves 4

INGREDIENTS

1 onion, chopped
5 garlic cloves, chopped
225 ml/8 fl oz/1 cup chicken or
  vegetable stock
2 tbsp vegetable oil
175 g/ 6 oz long-grain rice
½ tsp ground cumin

225 ml/8 fl oz/1 cup liquid from
  cooking black beans (including
  some black beans, too)
salt and pepper

TO GARNISH:
3–5 spring onions (scallions), thinly
  sliced
2 tbsp chopped fresh coriander
  (cilantro) leaves

1 Put the onion in a blender with the garlic and stock and blend until the consistency of a chunky sauce.

2 Heat the oil in a heavy-based pan and cook the rice until it is golden. Add the onion mixture, with the cooking liquid from the black beans (and any beans, too). Add the cumin, with salt and pepper to taste

3 Cover the pan and cook over a medium-low heat for about 10 minutes or until the rice is just tender. The rice should be a greyish colour and taste delicious.

4 Fluff up the rice with a fork, and leave to rest for about 5 minutes, covered. Serve sprinkled with thinly sliced spring onions (scallions) and chopped coriander (cilantro).

VARIATION

Instead of black beans, use pinto beans or chick-peas (garbanzo beans). Proceed as above and serve with any savoury spicy sauce, or as an accompaniment to roasted meat.

Lentils Simmered with Fruit

Although this might seem an unusual combination, when you spoon up this traditional dish you'll see how the fruit lightens the earthy lentils, to create a delicious side dish.

Serves 4

INGREDIENTS

125 g/4½ oz brown or green lentils
about 1 litre/1¾ pints/4 cups water
2 tbsp vegetable oil
3 small to medium onions, chopped
4 garlic cloves, coarsely chopped
1 large tart apple, roughly chopped

about ¼ ripe pineapple, skin removed
  and roughly chopped
2 tomatoes, deseeded and diced
1 almost ripe banana, cut into
  bite-sized pieces
salt

cayenne pepper, to taste
fresh parsley sprig, to garnish

1 Combine the lentils with the water in a pan, then bring to the boil. Reduce the heat and simmer over a low heat for about 40 minutes until the lentils are tender. Do not let them get mushy.

2 Meanwhile, heat the oil in a frying pan (skillet) and fry the onions and garlic until lightly browned and softened. Add the apple and continue to cook until golden. Add the pineapple, heat through, stirring, then add the tomatoes. Cook over a medium heat until thickened, stirring occasionally

3 Drain the lentils, reserving 120 ml/4 fl oz/1 cup of the cooking liquid. Add the drained lentils to the sauce, stirring in the reserved liquid if necessary. Heat through for a minute to mingle the flavours.

4 Add the banana to the pan, then season with salt and cayenne pepper. Serve garnished with parsley.

VARIATION

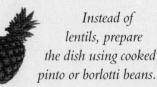

Instead of lentils, prepare the dish using cooked pinto or borlotti beans.

Dry Soup
of Thin Noodles

This curiously named baked dish is made with pasta, tortillas or rice, and has an appetising dense texture. It often has a cheesy topping, and is served either as a first course, such as an Italian might, or as a comforting supper dish.

Serves 4

INGREDIENTS

350 g/12 very thin pasta, such as
   fideo or capellini
2–3 bay leaves
2–3 chorizo sausages
1 onion, chopped
1 green (bell) pepper or mild green
   chilli, such as anaheim or poblano,
   deseeded and chopped

4–5 garlic cloves, finely chopped
350 ml/12 fl oz/1½ cups tomato
   passata
350 ml/12 fl oz/1½ cups hot chicken,
   meat or vegetable stock
¼ tsp ground cumin
½ tsp mild red chilli powder
pinch of dried oregano leaves

350 g/12 oz grated sharp cheese
2 tbsp chopped fresh coriander
   (cilantro)

1 Boil the pasta in boiling salted water with the bay leaves. Drain and discard the bay leaves. Rinse the noodles to rid them of excess starch. Leave to drain.

2 Fry the chorizo in a frying pan (skillet). When it begins to brown, add the onion, (bell) pepper and garlic, then continue to cook, stirring occasionally, until the vegetables are softened.

3 Add the tomato passata, stock, cumin, chilli and oregano and remove from the heat.

4 Toss the pasta with the hot sauce, then transfer to an ovenproof dish. Level the surface with a spoon, then cover with a layer of the grated cheese.

5 Bake in a preheated oven at 200°C/400°F/Gas Mark 6 for about 15 minutes until the top is lightly browned and the pasta is heated through. Serve at once, sprinkled with the chopped fresh coriander (cilantro).

Main Courses

In Mexico the main meal is traditionally served at midday, a gloriously relaxed affair, with usually a fish or meat dish for the central course. Using a wonderful mix of flavours and cooking methods, a result of Mexico's complex and colourful past, the cuisine offers some delicious main dishes, full of spicy tastes.

Eggs are cooked with spices, tangy herbs, garlic and tomatoes to make an appetizing topping to tortillas, while fish is given a lift with subtle spicy marinades – salmon grilled with a smoky chilli dressing or snapper baked with lime and coriander (cilantro) is a feast of Mexican flavours.

Sizzling strips of beef rolled up with crunchy vegetables in a tortilla is classic Mexican fare, as is pork stewed with mild chillies, sweet plantains and potatoes – an inspiring marriage of flavours and textures. Or try the classic Mexican way of simmering pork until meltingly tender, then frying it until crisp and golden. Cook chicken with Mexican flair by stewing it with vegetables and fruit, or marinate chicken wings in tequila, to tenderise and add flavour for barbecuing.

Serve any of the dishes in this chapter to bring a touch of sunny Mexico to your meals, whether it is a family lunch or a dinner with friends.

Jalisco-style Eggs

This hearty breakfast dish from Jalisco is a classic Mexican way of serving eggs – a feast of flavours!

Serves 4

INGREDIENTS

4 corn tortillas
1 avocado
lime or lemon juice, for tossing
175 g/6 oz chorizo sausage, sliced or
    diced

2 tbsp butter or water, for cooking
4 eggs
4 tbsp feta or Wensleydale cheese,
    crumbled
salsa of your choice

1 tbsp chopped fresh coriander
    (cilantro)
1 tbsp finely chopped spring onions
    (scallions)

1 Heat the tortillas in an ungreased non-stick frying pan (skillet), sprinkling them with a few drops of water as they heat; wrap the tortillas in a clean tea towel (dish cloth) as you work to keep them warm. Alternatively, heat through in a stack in the pan, alternating the top and bottom tortillas so that they warm evenly. Wrap to keep warm.

2 Cut the avocado in half around the stone (pit). Twist apart, then remove the stone (pit) with a knife. Carefully peel off the skin, dice the flesh and toss in lime or lemon juice to prevent discoloration.

3 Brown the chorizo sausage in a pan, then arrange on each warmed tortilla. Keep warm.

4 Meanwhile, heat the butter or water in the non-stick frying pan (skillet), break in an egg and cook until the white is set but the yolk still soft. Remove from the pan and place on top of one tortilla. Keep warm.

5 Cook the remaining eggs in the same way, adding to the tortillas.

6 Arrange the avocado, cheese and a spoonful of salsa on each tortilla. Add the fresh coriander (cilantro) and spring onions (scallions) and serve.

Migas

A wonderful brunch or late-night supper dish, this is made by scrambling egg with chillies, tomatoes and crisp tortilla chips.

Serves 4

INGREDIENTS

2 tbsp butter
6 garlic cloves, finely chopped
1 fresh green chilli, such as jalapeño
  or serrano, deseeded and diced
1½ tsp ground cumin

6 ripe tomatoes, coarsely chopped
8 eggs, lightly beaten
8–10 corn tortillas, cut into strips and
  fried until crisp, or an equal amount
  of not too salty tortilla chips

4 tbsp chopped fresh coriander
  (cilantro)
3–4 spring onions (scallions), thinly
  sliced
mild chilli powder, to garnish

1 Melt half the butter in a pan. Add the garlic and chilli and cook until softened, but not browned. Add the cumin and cook for 30 seconds, stirring, then add the tomatoes and cook over a medium heat for a further 3–4 minutes, or until the tomato juices have evaporated. Remove from the pan and set aside.

2 Melt the remaining butter in a frying pan (skillet) over a low heat and pour in the beaten eggs. Cook, stirring, until the eggs begin to set.

3 Add the reserved chilli tomato mixture, stirring gently to mix into the eggs.

4 Carefully add the tortilla strips or chips and continue cooking, stirring once or twice, until the eggs are the consistency you wish. The tortillas should be pliable and chewy.

5 Transfer to a serving plate and surround with the fresh coriander (cilantro) and spring onions. Garnish with a sprinkling of mild chilli powder and serve.

COOK'S TIP

Serve the migas with soured cream or crème fraîche on top, to melt seductively into the spicy eggs.

VARIATION

Add browned minced (ground) beef or pork to the softly scrambling egg mixture at Step 3. A bunch of cooked, chopped, spinach or chard can be stirred in as well, to add fresh colour.

Eggs Oaxaca Style

Cooking eggs in a flat omelette, then cutting them into strips and simmering them in a spicy sauce makes an unusual dish for brunch or dinner.

Serves 4

INGREDIENTS

1 kg/2 lb 4 oz ripe tomatoes
about 12 small button onions, halved
8 garlic cloves, whole and unpeeled
2 fresh mild green chillies
pinch of ground cumin

pinch of dried oregano,
pinch of sugar, if needed
2–3 tsp vegetable oil
8 eggs, lightly beaten
1–2 tbsp tomato purée (paste)

salt and pepper
1–2 tbsp chopped fresh coriander
(cilantro), to garnish

1 Heat an ungreased heavy-based frying pan (skillet), add the tomatoes and char lightly, turning them once or twice. Allow to cool.

2 Meanwhile lightly char the onions, garlic and chillies in the pan. Allow to cool slightly.

3 Cut the cooled tomatoes into pieces and place in a blender or food processor, with their charred skins. Remove the stems and seeds from the chillies, then peel and chop. Remove the skins from the garlic, then chop. Roughly chop the onions. Add the chillies, garlic and onions to the tomatoes.

4 Process to make a rough purée, then add the cumin and oregano. Season with salt and pepper to taste, and add sugar if needed.

5 Heat the oil in a non-stick frying pan (skillet), add a ladleful of egg and cook to make a thin omelette. Continue to make omelettes, stacking them on a plate as they are cooked. Slice into noodle-like ribbons.

6 Bring the sauce to the boil, adjust the seasoning, adding tomato purée (paste) to taste. Add the omelette strips, warm through and serve at once, garnished with a sprinkling of fresh coriander (cilantro).

Eggs with Refried Beans

In the Yucatan, this classic dish would be sandwiched between two crisp tortillas, but layering it all on top of one tortilla looks much more festive.

Serves 4

INGREDIENTS

400 g/14 oz tomatoes, skinned and chopped
1 onion, chopped
1 garlic clove, finely chopped
½ fresh green chilli, such as jalapeño or serrano, deseeded and chopped
¼ tsp ground cumin
2 tbsp extra-virgin olive oil
1 plantain, peeled and diced

1 tbsp butter
4 corn tortillas, warmed or fried crisply into a tostada
about 400 g/14 oz can refried beans, warmed with 2 tbsp of water
2 tbsp water or butter
8 eggs
1 red (bell) pepper, grilled (broiled), peeled, deseeded and cut into strips

3–4 tbsp cooked green peas, at room temperature
4–6 tbsp diced cooked or smoked ham
50–75 g/2–3 oz crumbled feta cheese
3 spring onions (scallions), thinly sliced
salt and pepper

1 Process the tomatoes in a blender or food processor with the onion, garlic, chilli, cumin, salt and pepper to a purée.

2 Heat the oil in a heavy-based frying pan (skillet), then ladle in a little of the sauce and cook until it reduces in volume and becomes almost paste-like. Continue adding and reducing the sauce in this way. Keep warm.

3 Brown the plantain in the butter in a heavy-based non-stick frying pan (skillet). Remove and set aside. Spread the tortillas with the refried beans and keep warm in a low oven.

4 Heat the water or butter in the frying pan (skillet), break in an egg and cook until the white is set but the yolk still soft. Remove from the pan and place

on top of one tortilla. Cook the remaining eggs in the same way, adding to the tortillas.

5 To serve, spoon the warm sauce around the eggs on each tortilla. Sprinkle over the diced plantain, (bell) pepper, peas, ham, feta cheese and spring onions (scallions). Season with salt and pepper to taste and serve immediately.

Fish with Yucatecan Flavours

Annatto seeds are rock hard little red seeds that need to be soaked overnight before you can grind them. They have a distinctive lemony flavour and impart a dark orange colour to the dish.

Serves 8

INGREDIENTS

4 tbsp annatto seeds, soaked in water overnight
3 garlic cloves, finely chopped
1 tbsp mild chilli powder
1 tbsp paprika
1 tsp ground cumin
½ tsp dried oregano

2 tbsp beer or tequila
juice of 1 lime and 1 orange or 3 tbsp pineapple juice
2 tbsp olive oil
2 tbsp chopped fresh coriander (cilantro)
¼ tsp ground cinnamon

¼ tsp ground cloves
1 kg/2 lb 4 oz swordfish steaks
banana leaves, for wrapping (optional)
fresh coriander (cilantro) leaves, to garnish
orange wedges, to serve

1 Drain the annatto, then crush them to a paste with a pestle and mortar. Work in the garlic, chilli powder, paprika, cumin, oregano, beer or tequila, fruit juice, olive oil, fresh coriander (cilantro), cinnamon and cloves.

2 Smear the paste on to the fish and marinate in the refrigerator for at least 3 hours or overnight.

3 Wrap the fish steaks in banana leaves, tying with string to make parcels. Bring water to the boil in a steamer, then add a batch of parcels to the top part of the steamer and cook for about 15 minutes or until the fish is cooked through.

4 Alternatively, cook the fish without wrapping in the banana leaves. To cook on the barbecue (grill), place in a hinged basket, or on a rack, and cook over the hot coals for 5–6 minutes on each side until cooked through.

Or cook the fish under a preheated grill (broiler) for 5–6 minutes on each side until cooked through.

5 Garnish with coriander (cilantro) and serve with orange wedges for squeezing over the fish.

Prawns (Shrimp) in Green Bean Sauce

The sweet briny flesh of prawns (shrimp) is wonderful paired
with the smoky scent of chipotle chilli.

Serves 4

INGREDIENTS

3 onions, chopped
5 garlic cloves, chopped
2 tbsp vegetable oil
5–7 ripe tomatoes, diced
175–225 g/6–8 oz green beans, cut
    into 5 cm/2 inch pieces and
    blanched for 1 minute

¼ tsp ground cumin
pinch of ground allspice
pinch of ground cinnamon
½–1 canned chipotle chilli in adobo
    marinade, with some of the
    marinade

450 ml/16 fl oz/2 cups fish stock or
    water mixed with a fish stock cube
450 g/1 lb raw prawns (shrimp),
    peeled
fresh coriander (cilantro) sprigs
1 lime, cut into wedges

1 Lightly fry the onions and garlic in the oil over a low heat for 5–10 minutes until softened. Add the tomatoes and cook for a further 2 minutes.

2 Add the green beans, cumin, allspice, cinnamon, the chipotle chilli and marinade and fish stock. Bring to the boil, then reduce the heat and simmer for a few minutes to combine the flavours.

3 Add the prawns (shrimp) and cook for 1–2 minutes only, then remove the pan from the heat and leave the prawns (shrimp) to steep in the hot liquid to finish cooking. They are cooked when they have turned a bright pink colour.

4 Serve the prawns (shrimp) immediately, garnished with the fresh coriander (cilantro) and accompanied by the lime wedges.

VARIATION

If you can find them, use bottled nopales (edible cactus), cut into strips, to add an exotic touch to the dish.

Mussels Cooked with Lager

Mussels cooked in beer, tomatoes and Mexican spices are great summertime fare.

Serves 4

INGREDIENTS

1.5 kg/3 lb 5 oz live mussels
450 ml/16 fl oz/2 cups lager
2 onions, chopped
5 garlic cloves, chopped coarsely

1 fresh green chilli, such as jalapeño or serrano, deseeded and thinly sliced

175 g/6 oz/²/₃ cup fresh tomatoes, diced, or canned chopped
2–3 tbsp chopped fresh coriander (cilantro)

1 Scrub the mussels under cold running water to remove any mud. Using a sharp knife, cut away the feathery 'beards' from the shells. Discard any open mussels that do not shut when tapped sharply with a knife. Rinse again in cold water.

2 Place the lager, onions, garlic, chilli and tomatoes in a heavy-based pan. Bring to the boil.

3 Add the mussels and cook, covered, over a medium-high heat for about 10 minutes until the shells open. Discard any mussels that do not open.

4 Ladle into individual bowls and serve sprinkled with fresh coriander.

VARIATION

Add the kernels of 2 corn-on-the-cobs to the lager mixture in Step 2. A pinch of sugar might be needed to bring out the sweetness of the corn.

Barbecued (Grilled) Clams with Sweetcorn Salsa

Cook with Mexican flair, and serve up clams from the barbecue (grill), topped with a spicy sweetcorn salsa.

Serves 4

INGREDIENTS

2 kg/4 lb 8 oz clams in their shells
5 ripe tomatoes
2 garlic cloves, finely chopped
225 g/8 oz can sweetcorn, drained

3 tbsp finely chopped fresh
coriander (cilantro)
3 spring onions (scallions), thinly
sliced
¼ tsp ground cumin

juice of ½ lime
½–1 fresh green chilli, deseeded and
finely chopped
salt
lime wedges, to serve

1 Place the clams in a large bowl. Cover with cold water and add a handful of salt. Leave to soak for 30 minutes to rinse out the sand and grit.

2 Meanwhile, skin the tomatoes. Place in a heatproof bowl, pour boiling water over to cover and stand for 30 seconds. Drain and plunge into cold water. The skins will then slide off easily. Cut the tomatoes in half, deseed, then chop the flesh.

3 To make the salsa, combine the tomatoes, garlic, sweetcorn, coriander (cilantro), spring onions (scallions), cumin, lime juice and chilli in a bowl. Season with salt to taste.

4 Drain the clams, discarding any that are open. Place the clams on the hot coals of a barbecue (grill), allowing about 5 minutes per side. They will pop open when they are ready. Discard any that do not open.

5 Immediately remove from the barbecue (grill), top with the salsa and serve with lime wedges for squeezing over the clams.

VARIATION

Mussels can be used in place of the clams very successfully.

Chilli-marinated Prawns (Shrimp) with Avocado Sauce

Avocado salsa is delicious spooned on to anything spicy from the grill (broiler) or barbecue (grill), especially seafood.

Serves 4

INGREDIENTS

650 g/1 lb 5 oz large prawns (shrimp), shelled
½ tsp ground cumin
½ tsp mild chilli powder
½ tsp paprika
2 tbsp orange juice

grated rind of 1 orange
2 tbsp extra-virgin olive oil
2 tbsp chopped fresh coriander (cilantro), plus extra for garnishing
2 ripe avocados

½ onion, finely chopped
¼ fresh green or red chilli, deseeded and chopped
juice of ½ lime
salt and pepper

1 Combine the prawns (shrimp) with the cumin, chilli powder, paprika, orange juice and rind, olive oil and half the coriander (cilantro). Season to taste.

2 Thread the prawns (shrimp) on to metal skewers, or bamboo skewers that have been soaked in cold water for 30 minutes.

3 Cut the avocados in half around the stone (pit). Twist apart, then remove the stone (pit) with a knife. Carefully peel off the skin, then dice the flesh. Immediately combine the avocados with the remaining coriander (cilantro), onion, chilli and lime juice. Season with salt and pepper and set aside.

4 Place the prawns (shrimp) on a hot barbecue (grill) and cook for only a few minutes on each side.

5 Serve the prawns (shrimp), garnished with coriander (cilantro) and accompanied by the avocado sauce.

VARIATION

For luscious sandwiches, toast crusty rolls, cut in half and buttered, over the hot coals and fill them with the cooked prawns (shrimp) and avocado sauce.

Squid Simmered with Tomatoes, Olives & Capers

This flavourful squid dish from Vera Cruz would be good with warmed flour tortillas, for do-it-yourself tacos.

Serves 4

INGREDIENTS

3 tbsp extra-virgin olive oil
900 g/2 lb cleaned squid, cut into
   rings and tentacles
1 onion, chopped
3 garlic cloves, chopped
400 g/14 oz can chopped tomatoes
½–1 fresh mildish green chilli,
   deseeded and chopped

1 tbsp finely chopped fresh parsley
¼ tsp chopped fresh thyme
¼ tsp chopped fresh oregano
¼ tsp chopped fresh marjoram
large pinch of ground cinnamon
large pinch of ground allspice
large pinch of sugar

15–20 pimiento-stuffed green olives,
   sliced
1 tbsp capers
salt and pepper
1 tbsp chopped fresh coriander
   (cilantro), to garnish

1 Heat the oil in a pan and lightly fry the squid until it turns opaque. Season with salt and pepper and remove from the pan with a slotted spoon.

2 Add the onion and garlic to the remaining oil in the pan and fry until softened. Stir in the tomatoes, chilli, herbs, cinnamon, allspice, sugar and

olives. Cover and cook over a medium-low heat for 5–10 minutes until the mixture thickens slightly. Uncover the pan and cook for a further 5 minutes to concentrate the flavours.

3 Stir in the reserved squid and any of the juices that have gathered. Add the capers and heat through.

4 Adjust the seasoning, then serve immediately, garnished with fresh coriander (cilantro).

Pan-fried Scallops Mexicana

Scallops, with their sweet flesh, are delicious with the rindy flavours of Mexico. Often they are prepared just this simply, served with wedges of lime to squeeze over as desired, and a stack of warm corn tortillas.

Serves 4–6

INGREDIENTS

2 tbsp butter
2 tbsp extra-virgin olive oil
650 g/1 lb 6 oz scallops, shelled
4–5 spring onions (scallions), thinly
   sliced

3–4 garlic cloves, finely chopped
½ fresh green chilli, deseeded and
   finely chopped
2 tbsp finely chopped fresh coriander
   (cilantro)

juice of ½ lime
salt and pepper
lime wedges, to serve

1 Heat half the butter and olive oil in a heavy-based frying pan (skillet) until the butter foams.

2 Add the scallops and cook quickly until just turning opaque; do not overcook. Remove from the pan with a slotted spoon and keep warm.

3 Add the remaining butter and oil to the pan, then toss in the spring onions (scallions) and garlic and cook over a medium heat until the spring onions (scallions) are wilted. Return the scallops to the pan.

4 Remove the pan from the heat and add the chopped chilli and coriander (cilantro). Squeeze in the juice from half a lime. Season with salt and pepper to taste and stir to mix well.

5 Serve immediately with lime wedges for squeezing over the scallops.

VARIATION

Mix leftover scallops with a little aioli or mayonnaise mixed with garlic and a little olive oil. Serve with roasted (bell) peppers on a bed of greens, with a handful of salty black olives for a taste of the Mediterranean, Mexico style.

Spicy Grilled (Broiled) Salmon

The woody smoked flavours of the chipotle chilli are delicious brushed on to salmon for grilling (broiling).

Serves 4

INGREDIENTS

4 salmon steaks, about
   175–225 g/6–8 oz each
lime slices, to garnish

MARINADE:
4 garlic cloves
2 tbsp extra-virgin olive oil
pinch of ground allspice

pinch of ground cinnamon
juice of 2 limes
1–2 tsp marinade from canned
   chipotle chillies or bottled chipotle
   chilli salsa
¼ tsp ground cumin
pinch of sugar
salt and pepper

TO SERVE:
tomato wedges
3 spring onions (scallions) finely
   chopped
shredded lettuce

1 To make the marinade, finely chop the garlic and place in a bowl with the olive oil, allspice, cinnamon, lime juice, chipotle marinade, cumin and sugar. Add salt and pepper and stir to combine.

2 Coat the salmon with the garlic mixture, then place in a non-metallic dish. Leave to marinate for at least an hour or overnight in the refrigerator.

3 Transfer to a grill (broiler) pan and cook under a preheated grill (broiler) for 3–4 minutes on each side. Alternatively, cook the salmon over hot coals on a barbecue (grill) until cooked through.

4 To serve, mix the tomato wedges with the spring onions (scallions). Place the salmon on individual plates and arrange the tomato salad and

shredded lettuce alongside. Garnish with lime slices and serve immediately.

VARIATION

The marinade also goes well with fresh tuna steaks.

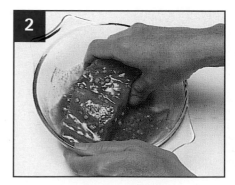

Fish Baked with Lime

Tangy and simple to prepare, this is excellent served with rice and beans for an easy lunch. Follow up with coffee ice cream topped with espresso beans and chocolate sauce.

Serves 4

INGREDIENTS

1 kg/2 lb 4 oz white fish fillets, such
  as bass, plaice or cod
1 lime, halved
3 tbsp extra-virgin olive oil
1 large onion, finely chopped

3 garlic cloves, finely chopped
2–3 pickled jalapeño chillies (see
  Cook's Tip), chopped
6–8 tbsp chopped fresh coriander
  (cilantro)

salt and pepper
lemon and lime wedges, to serve

1 Place the fish fillets in a bowl and sprinkle with salt and pepper. Squeeze the juice from the lime over the fish.

2 Heat the olive oil in a frying pan (skillet). Add the onion and garlic and fry for about 2 minutes, stirring frequently, until softened. Remove from the heat.

3 Place a third of the onion mixture and a little of the chillies and coriander (cilantro) in the bottom of a shallow baking dish or roasting tin (pan). Arrange the fish on top. Top with the remaining onion mixture, chillies and coriander (cilantro).

4 Bake in a preheated oven at 180°C/350°F/Gas Mark 4 for about 15–20 minutes or until the fish has become slightly opaque and firm to the touch. Serve at once, with lemon and lime wedges for squeezing over the fish.

COOK'S TIP

Pickled jalapeños are called jalapeños en escabeche *and are available from specialist stores.*

VARIATION

Add sliced flavourful fresh tomatoes, or canned chopped tomatoes, to the onion mixture at the end of Step 2.

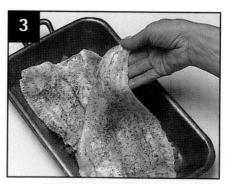

Lobster Cooked Rosarita Beach Style

Barbecuing (grilling) gives lobsters a lovely smoky scent that is enhanced by spicy red chilli.
Serve with creamy refried beans and a stack of warm corn tortillas and
pretend you're on Rosarita Beach in Baja California!

Serves 4

INGREDIENTS

2–4 cooked lobsters, depending on their size, cut through the middle into two halves, or 4 lobster tails, the meat loosened slightly from its shell

CHILLI BUTTER:
115 g/4 oz unsalted butter, softened
3–4 tbsp chopped fresh coriander (cilantro)
about 5 garlic cloves, chopped
2–3 tbsp mild chilli powder
juice of ½ lime
salt and pepper

TO SERVE:
400 g/14 oz refried beans, warmed with 2 tbsp water
chopped spring onions (scallions)
lime wedges
salsa of your choice

1 To make the chilli butter, put the butter in a bowl and mix in the coriander (cilantro), garlic, chilli powder and lime juice. Add salt and pepper.

2 Rub the chilli butter into the cut side of the lobster or the lobster tails, working it into all the lobsters cracks and crevices.

3 Wrap loosely in kitchen foil and place, cut-side up, on a rack over the hot coals of a barbecue (grill). Cook for 15 minutes or until heated through.

4 Serve with warm refried beans, topped with chopped spring onions (scallions), plus lime wedges and salsa.

COOK'S TIP

The flavoured butter is also delicious with grilled (broiled) fish steaks and large prawns (shrimp).

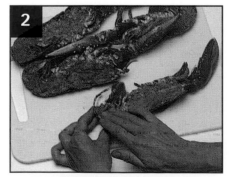
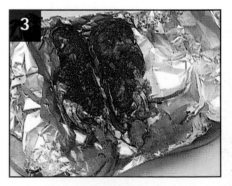

Ropa Vieja

*Fill warmed tortillas with this tender, browned beef and a selection of
crisp vegetables to make wonderful tacos*

Serves 6

INGREDIENTS

1.5 kg/3 lb 5 oz flank beef steak or
   other stewing meat
beef stock
1 carrot, sliced
10 garlic cloves, sliced
2 tbsp vegetable oil
2 onions, thinly sliced

3–4 mild fresh green chillies, such as
   anaheim or poblano, deseeded and
   sliced
warmed flour tortillas, to serve

SALAD GARNISHES:
3 ripe tomatoes, diced
8–10 radishes, diced
3–4 tbsp chopped fresh coriander
   (cilantro)
4–5 spring onions (scallions), chopped
1–2 limes, cut into wedges

1 Put the meat in a large pan
and cover with a mixture of
stock and water. Add the carrot
and half the garlic with salt and
pepper to taste. Cover and bring
to the boil, then reduce the heat
to low. Skim the scum from the
surface, then re-cover the pan and
cook the meat gently for about 2
hours until very tender.

2 Remove the pan from the
heat and leave the meat to
cool in the liquid. When cool
enough to handle, remove from
the liquid and shred with your
fingers and a fork.

3 Heat the oil in a large
frying pan (skillet), add the
remaining garlic, onions and
chillies and fry until lightly
coloured. Remove from the pan
and set aside.

4 Add the meat to the pan and
cook over a medium-high
heat until browned and crisp.

Transfer to a serving dish. Top
with the onion mixture and
surround with the tomatoes,
radishes, coriander (cilantro),
spring onions (scallions) and lime
wedges. Serve with warmed
tortillas.

Classic Beef Fajitas

Sizzling marinated strips of meat rolled up in soft flour tortillas with a tangy salsa is a real Mexican treat, perfect for relaxed entertaining.

Serves 4–6

INGREDIENTS

700 g/1 lb 9 oz beef skirt steak or
  other tender steak, cut into strips
6 garlic cloves, chopped
juice of 1 lime
large pinch of mild chilli powder
large pinch of paprika
large pinch of ground cumin
1–2 tbsp extra-virgin olive oil
12 flour tortillas

vegetable oil, for frying
1–2 avocados, stoned (pitted), sliced
  and tossed with lime juice
120 ml/4 fl oz/½ cup soured cream
salt and pepper

PICO DE GALLO SALSA:
8 ripe tomatoes, diced
3 spring onions (scallions), sliced

1–2 fresh green chillies, such as
  jalapeño or serrano, deseeded and
  chopped
3–4 tbsp chopped fresh coriander
  (cilantro)
5–8 radishes, diced
ground cumin

1 Combine the beef with half the garlic, half the lime juice, the chilli powder, paprika, cumin and olive oil. Add salt and pepper, mix well and leave to marinate for at least 30 minutes at room temperature, or up to overnight in the refrigerator.

2 To make the pico de gallo salsa, put the tomatoes in a bowl with the spring onions (scallions), green chilli, coriander and radishes. Season to taste with cumin, salt and pepper. Set aside.

3 Heat the tortillas in a lightly greased non-stick frying pan (skillet); wrap in kitchen foil as you work, to keep them warm.

4 Stir-fry the meat in a little oil over a high heat until browned and just cooked through.

5 Serve the sizzling hot meat with the warm tortillas, the pico de gallo salsa, avocado and soured cream for each person to make his or her own rolled up fajitas.

COOK'S TIP

A lettuce and orange salad makes a refreshing accompaniment.

Michoacan Beef

*This rich smoky flavoured stew is delicious; leftovers
make a great filling for tacos, too!*

Serves 4–6

INGREDIENTS

about 3 tbsp plain (all-purpose) flour

1 kg/2 lb 4 oz stewing beef, cut into
    large bite-sized pieces

2 tbsp vegetable oil

2 onions, chopped

5 garlic cloves, chopped

400 g/14 oz tomatoes, diced

1½ dried chipotle chillies,

reconstituted (see page 100),
deseeded and cut into thin strips, or
a few shakes of bottled chipotle
salsa

1.5 litres/2¾ pints/6¼ cups beef
stock

350 g/12 oz green beans, topped and
tailed

a pinch of sugar

salt and pepper

TO SERVE:
simmered beans
cooked rice

1 Place the flour in a large
bowl and season with salt
and pepper. Add the beef and
toss to coat well. Remove from
the bowl, shaking off the excess
flour.

2 Heat the oil in a frying pan
(skillet) and brown the meat
briefly over a high heat. Reduce
the heat to medium, add the
onions and garlic and cook for
a further 2 minutes.

3 Add the tomatoes, chillies
and stock, then cover and
simmer over a low heat for 1½
hours or until the meat is very
tender, adding the green beans
15 minutes before the end of the
cooking time. Skim off any fat
that rises to the surface, every
now and again.

4 Transfer to individual bowls
and serve with simmered
beans and rice.

COOK'S TIP

*This is traditionally made
with nopales, edible cactus,
which gives the dish a
distinctive flavour. Look out
for them in specialist stores.
For this recipe you need 350–
400 g/12–14 oz can nopales, or
fresh nopales, peeled, sliced and
blanched. Add them with the
tomatoes at Step 3.*

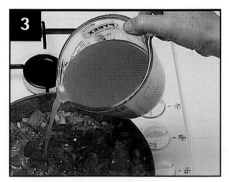

Chillies Stuffed with Spicy Beef

Large mildish-tasting green chillies are roasted, peeled and stuffed with a succulent meat mixture that is sweet, spicy and punctuated with nuts.

Serves 4

INGREDIENTS

4 large fresh poblano chillies
flour for dusting
vegetable oil, for frying
Quick Tomato Sauce (see page 82),
  to serve

SPICY BEEF FILLING:
500 g/1 lb 2 oz minced (ground) beef
1 onion, finely chopped
2–3 garlic cloves, finely chopped

50 ml/2 fl oz/¼ cup dry or sweet
  sherry
pinch of ground cinnamon
pinch of ground cloves
pinch of ground cumin
400 g/14 oz can chopped tomatoes
1–3 tsp sugar
1 tbsp vinegar
3 tbsp chopped fresh coriander
  (cilantro)

2–3 tbsp coarsely chopped toasted
  almonds
salt and pepper

BATTER:
6–8 Tbsp plain (all purpose) flour
3 eggs, separated
120 ml/4 fl oz/½ cup water

1 Roast the chillies under a preheated grill (broiler) until the skin is charred. Place in a plastic bag, seal well and leave to stand for 20 minutes. Make a slit in the side of each chilli and remove the seeds, leaving the stems intact. Set aside.

2 Brown the meat and onion together in a heavy-based frying pan (skillet) over a medium heat. Pour off any extra fat, then add the garlic and sherry and boil down until the liquid has nearly evaporated.

3 Season with salt, pepper, cinnamon, cloves and cumin, then add the tomatoes, sugar and vinegar and cook over a medium heat until the tomatoes have reduced to a thick, strongly flavoured sauce.

4 Stir in the chopped fresh coriander (cilantro) and almonds and heat through. Stuff as much of this filling into the chillies as will fit, then dust each with flour. Set aside.

5 Lightly beat the yolks with the flour, a pinch of salt and enough water to make a thick batter. Whisk the egg whites until they form stiff peaks. Fold the egg whites into the batter mixture, then gently dip each stuffed chilli into the batter.

6 Heat the oil in a deep frying pan (skillet) until very hot and just smoking. Gently fry the chillies until they are golden brown. Serve hot, topped with the tomato sauce.

Spicy Pork with Prunes

Prunes add an earthy, wine flavour to this spicy stew.
Serve with tortillas or crusty bread to dip into the rich sauce.

Serves 4–6

INGREDIENTS

1.5 kg/3 lb 5 oz pork joint, such as leg
  or shoulder
juice of 2–3 limes
10 garlic cloves, chopped
3–4 tbsp mild chilli powder, such as
  ancho or New Mexico
4 tbsp vegetable oil

2 onions, chopped
500 ml/18 fl oz/2¼ cups chicken
  stock
25 small tart tomatoes, roughly
  chopped
25 prunes, stoned (pitted)
1–2 tsp sugar

about a pinch of ground cinnamon
about a pinch of ground allspice
about a pinch of ground cumin
salt
warmed corn tortillas, to serve

1 Combine the pork with the lime juice, garlic, chilli powder, 2 tablespoons of oil and salt. Leave to marinate in the refrigerator overnight.

2 Remove the pork from the marinade. Wipe the pork dry with paper towels and reserve the marinade. Heat the remaining oil in a flameproof casserole and brown the pork evenly until just golden. Add the onions, the reserved marinade and stock.

Cover and cook in a preheated oven at 180°C/350°F/Gas Mark 4 for about 2–3 hours until tender.

3 Spoon off fat from the surface of the cooking liquid and add the tomatoes. Continue to cook for about 20 minutes until the tomatoes are tender. Mash the tomatoes into a coarse purée. Add the prunes and sugar, then adjust the seasoning, adding cinnamon, allspice and cumin to taste, as well as extra chilli powder, if wished.

4 Increase the oven temperature to 200°C/400°F/Gas Mark 6 and return the meat and sauce to the oven for a further 20–30 minutes or until the meat has browned on top and the juices have thickened.

5 Remove the meat from the pan and let it stand for a few minutes. Carefully carve it into thin slices and spoon the sauce over the top. Serve warm, with corn tortillas.

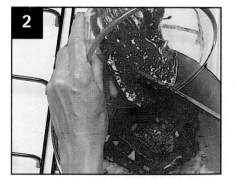
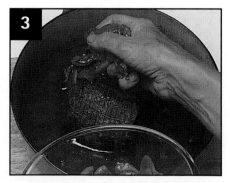

Red Mole of Pork & Red Chillies

Plantain and sesame seeds add a delicious hint of sweetness to this fragrant stew of pork and mild chillies, while potatoes add a satisfying chunky texture.

Serves 6

INGREDIENTS

1.25 kg/2 lb 12 oz pork shoulder or
   lean belly, cut into bite-sized pieces
1 onion, chopped
1 whole garlic bulb
2 bay leaves
1–2 stock cubes
6 dried ancho chillies

6 guajillo chillies
3–5 ripe big flavourful tomatoes
¼ tsp ground cloves
¼ tsp ground allspice
80 g/3 oz sesame seeds, toasted
1 large ripe plantain or banana,
   peeled and diced

3 tbsp vegetable oil
6–8 waxy potatoes, cut into chunks
3 tbsp yerba santa, or a combination
   of chopped fresh mint, oregano and
   coriander (cilantro)
1 cinnamon stick
salt and pepper

1 Place the pork in a large pan with the onion, the garlic, bay leaves and salt and pepper. Fill with cold water to the top.

2 Bring to the boil, then reduce the heat to a slow simmer. Skim off the scum, then stir in the stock cubes and cook the meat, covered, for about 3 hours until very tender.

3 Meanwhile, lightly roast the chillies in an ungreased

heavy-based frying pan (skillet) until they just change colour. Put them in a bowl and cover with boiling water. Cover and leave to soften for 20–30 minutes.

4 Roast the tomatoes in the frying pan (skillet), to brown the bases, then char the tops under a hot grill (broiler). Leave to cool.

5 When the chillies are softened, remove the stems and seeds, then purée them with

enough liquid to make a paste. Add the roasted tomatoes, cloves and allspice, with two-thirds of the sesame seeds and the plantain. Purée until smooth.

6 Remove the meat from the pan and reserve. Skim the fat from the surface of the stock.

7 Heat the oil in a pan, add the tomato purée mixture and cook for about 10 minutes until thickened. Do not let it burn. Add the potatoes and the herbs, with enough of the stock to keep the potatoes covered in sauce. Add the cinnamon stick.

8 Cook, covered, until the potatoes are tender, then add the reserved meat and heat through. Serve in bowls, sprinkled with the reserved sesame seeds.

Chile Verde

If tomatillos are not available, use fresh tomatoes and bottled green salsa instead, and add a good hit of lime juice at the end.

Serves 4

INGREDIENTS

1 kg/2 lb 4 oz pork, cut into bite-sized chunks
1 onion, chopped
2 bay leaves
1 whole garlic bulb, cut in half
1 stock cube
2 garlic cloves, chopped
450 g/1 lb oz fresh tomatillos, husks removed, cooked in a small amount of water until just tender, then chopped, or canned
2 large fresh mild green chillies, such as anaheim, or a combination of 1 green (bell) pepper and 2 jalapeño chillies, deseeded and chopped
3 tbsp vegetable oil
225 ml/8 fl oz/1 cup pork or chicken stock
½ tsp mild chilli powder, such as ancho or New Mexico
½ tsp cumin
4–6 tbsp chopped fresh coriander (cilantro), to garnish

TO SERVE:
warmed flour tortillas
lime wedges

1 Place the pork in a large pan with the onion, bay leaves and garlic bulb. Add water to cover and bring to the boil. Skim off the scum from the surface, reduce the heat to very low and simmer gently for about 1½ hours or until the meat is very tender.

2 Meanwhile, put the chopped garlic in a blender or food processor with the tomatillos and green chillies and (bell) pepper, if using. Process to a purée.

3 Heat the oil in a pan, add the tomatillo mixture and cook over a medium-high heat for about 10 minutes or until thickened. Add the stock, chilli powder and cumin.

4 When the meat is tender, remove from the pan and add to the sauce. Simmer gently to combine the flavours.

5 Garnish with the chopped coriander (cilantro) and serve with warmed tortillas and lime wedges.

Meatballs in Spicy-sweet Sauce

*Called albondigas in Mexican, these tasty meatballs are set off brilliantly against
the rich sauce and golden sweet potatoes.*

Serves 4

INGREDIENTS

225 g/8 oz minced (ground) pork
225 g/8 oz minced (ground) beef or
   lamb
6 tbsp cooked rice or finely crushed
   tortilla chips
1 egg, lightly beaten
1½ onions, finely chopped
5 garlic cloves, finely chopped
½ tsp ground cumin

large pinch of ground cinnamon
2 tbsp raisins
1 tbsp molasses sugar
1–2 tbsp cider or wine vinegar
400 g/14 oz can tomatoes, drained
   and chopped
350 ml/12 fl oz/1½ cups beef stock
1–2 tbsp mild chilli or ancho chilli
   powder

1 tbsp paprika
1 tbsp chopped fresh coriander
   (cilantro)
1 tbsp chopped fresh parsley or mint
2 tbsp vegetable oil
2 sweet potatoes, peeled and cut into
   small bite-sized chunks
salt and pepper
grated cheese, to serve

1 Mix thoroughly the meat with the rice or crushed tortilla chips, the egg, half the onion, half the garlic, the cumin, cinnamon and raisins.

2 Divide the mixture into even-sized pieces and roll into balls. Fry the balls in a non-stick frying pan (skillet) over a medium heat, adding a tiny bit of oil, if necessary, to help them brown. Remove the balls from the pan and set aside. Wipe the frying pan (skillet) clean.

3 Place the molasses sugar in a blender or food processor, with the vinegar, tomatoes, stock, chilli powder, paprika and remaining onion and garlic. Process together until blended, then stir in the chopped fresh herbs. Set aside.

4 Heat the oil in the cleaned frying pan (skillet), add the sweet potatoes and cook until tender and golden brown. Pour in the blended sauce and add the meatballs to the pan. Cook for about 10 minutes until the meatballs are heated through and the flavours have completlely combined. Season with salt and pepper. Serve accompanied with grated cheese.

Carnitas

In this classic Mexican dish, pieces of pork are first simmered to make them meltingly tender, then browned until irresistibly crisp.

Serves 4–6

INGREDIENTS

1 kg/2 lb 4 oz pork, such as
   lean belly
1 onion, chopped
1 whole garlic bulb, cut in half
½ tsp ground cumin
2 meat stock cubes

2 bay leaves
vegetable oil, for frying
salt and pepper
fresh chilli strips, to garnish

TO SERVE:
cooked rice
refried beans (see page 144)
salsa of your choice

1 Place the pork in a heavy-based pan with the onion, garlic, cumin, stock cubes and bay leaves. Add water to cover. Bring to the boil, then reduce the heat to very low. Skim off the foam and scum that has formed on the surface of the liquid.

2 Continue to cook very gently for about 2 hours or until the meat is tender. Remove from the heat and leave the meat to cool in the liquid.

3 Remove the meat from the pan with a slotted spoon. Cut off any rind (roast separately to make crackling). Cut the meat into bite-sized pieces and sprinkle with salt and pepper. Reserve 300 ml/10 fl oz/1¼ cups of the cooking liquid.

4 Brown the meat in a heavy-based frying pan (skillet) for about 15 minutes, to cook out the fat. Add the reserved meat cooking liquid and allow to reduce down. Continue to cook the meat for 15 minutes, covering the pan to avoid splattering. Turn the meat every now and again.

5 Transfer the meat to a serving dish, garnish with chilli strips and serve with rice, refried beans and salsa.

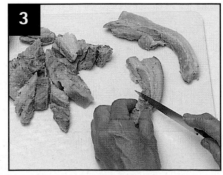

Spicy Meat & Chipotle Hash

This speciality from the town of Puebla in Mexico makes divine soft tacos: simply serve with a stack of warm soft corn tortillas and let everyone roll their own, fajita-style.

Serves 6

INGREDIENTS

1 tbsp vegetable oil
1 onion, finely chopped
450 g/1 lb leftover meat, such as
  simmered pork or beef, cooled and
  cut into thin strips
1 tbsp mild chilli powder
2 ripe tomatoes, deseeded and diced

about 225 ml/8 fl oz/1 cup meat
  stock
½–1 canned chipotle chillies, mashed,
  plus a little of the marinade, or a
  few shakes bottled chipotle salsa
120 ml/4 fl oz/½ cup soured cream
4–6 tbsp chopped fresh coriander

4–6 tbsp chopped radishes
3–4 leaves crisp lettuce, such as cos
  (romaine), shredded

1 Heat the oil in a frying pan (skillet), add the onion and cook until softened, stirring occasionally. Add the meat and sauté for about 3 minutes, stirring, until lightly browned.

2 Add the chilli powder, tomatoes and stock and cook until the tomatoes reduce to a sauce; mash the meat a bit as it cooks.

3 Add the chipotle chillies and continue to cook and mash until the sauce and meat are nearly blended.

4 Serve the dish with a stack of warmed corn tortillas so that people can fill them with the meaty mixture to make tacos. Also serve soured cream, fresh coriander, radishes and lettuce for each person to add to the meat.

COOK'S TIP

Avocados add an interesting texture contrast to the spicy meat – serve with 2 sliced avocados, tossed with lime juice. Try serving on top of tostada, crisply fried tortillas, instead of wrapping taco-style.

Simmered Stew of Meat, Chicken, Vegetables & Fruit

A big pot of cocido *is warming on a cold day, great for a family meal. Serve with a selection of several salsas, a stack of corn tortillas and a bowl of rice.*

Serves 6–8

INGREDIENTS

900 g/2 lb boneless pork, either in one
   joint or in pieces
2 bay leaves
1 onion, chopped
8 garlic cloves, finely chopped
2 tbsp chopped fresh coriander
   (cilantro)
1 carrot, thinly sliced
2 celery sticks, diced

2 chicken stock cubes
½ chicken, cut into portions
4–5 ripe tomatoes, diced
½ tsp mild chilli powder
grated rind of ¼ orange
¼ tsp ground cumin
juice of 3 oranges
1 courgette (zucchini), cut into bite-
   sized pieces

¼ cabbage, thinly sliced and blanched
1 apple, cut into bite-sized pieces
about 10 prunes, stoned (pitted)
¼ tsp ground cinnamon
pinch of dried ginger
2 hard chorizo sausages, about
   350 g/12 oz in total, cut into
   bite-sized pieces
salt and pepper

1 Combine the pork, bay leaves, onion, garlic, coriander (cilantro), carrot and celery in a large pan and fill with cold water. Bring to the boil, skim off the scum on the surface. Reduce heat and simmer gently for an hour.

2 Add the stock cubes to the pan, along with the chicken, tomatoes, chilli powder, orange rind and cumin. Continue to cook for a further 45 minutes or until the chicken is tender. Spoon off the fat that forms on the top of the liquid.

3 Add the orange juice, courgette (zucchini), cabbage, apple, prunes, cinnamon, ginger and chorizo. Continue to simmer for a further 20 minutes or until the courgette (zucchini) is soft and tender and the chorizo cooked through.

4 Season the stew with salt and pepper to taste. Serve immediately with rice, tortillas and salsa.

Chicken Breasts in Green Salsa with Soured Cream

Chicken breasts bathed in a fragrant sauce make a delicate dish, perfect for dinner parties. Serve with rice to complete the meal.

Serves 4

INGREDIENTS

4 chicken breast fillets
flour, for dredging
2–3 tbsp butter or combination
   butter and oil
450 g/1 lb mild green salsa or
   puréed tomatillos
225 ml/8 fl oz /1 cup
   chicken stock

1–2 garlic cloves, finely chopped
3–5 tbsp chopped fresh coriander
   (cilantro)
½ fresh green chilli, deseeded and
   chopped
½ tsp ground cumin
salt and pepper

TO SERVE:
225 ml/8 fl oz/1 cup soured cream
several leaves cos (romaine) lettuce,
   shredded
3–5 spring onions (scallions), thinly
   sliced
coarsely chopped fresh coriander
   (cilantro)

1 Sprinkle the chicken with salt and pepper, then dredge in flour. Shake off the excess.

2 Melt the butter in a frying pan (skillet), add the chicken and cook over a medium-high heat, turning once, until they are golden but not cooked through – they will continue to cook slightly in the sauce. Remove from pan and set aside.

3 Place the salsa, chicken stock, garlic, coriander (cilantro), chilli and cumin in a pan and bring to the boil. Reduce the heat to a low simmer. Add the chicken breasts to the sauce, spooning the sauce over the chicken. Continue to cook until the chicken is cooked through.

4 Remove the chicken from the pan and season with salt and pepper to taste. Serve with the soured cream, shredded lettuce, sliced spring onions (scallions) and chopped fresh coriander leaves.

Chicken with Yucatecan Vinegar Sauce

A paste of roasted garlic and mixed spices gives its evocative flavour to this tangy dish of simmered chicken, a speciality of Valladolid in the Yucatan peninsula.

Serves 4–6

INGREDIENTS

8 small boned chicken thighs
chicken stock
15–20 garlic cloves, unpeeled
1 tsp cumin seeds, lightly toasted
1 tsp coarsely ground black pepper
½ tsp ground cloves
2 tsp crumbled dried oregano or ½
   tsp crushed or powdered bay leaves

about ½ tsp salt
1 tbsp lime juice
1 tbsp flour, plus extra for dredging
   the chicken

3–4 onions, thinly sliced
2 fresh chillies, preferably mildish
   yellow ones, such as Mexican Guero
   or similar Turkish or Greek chillies,
   deseeded and sliced
120 ml/4 fl oz /1 cup vegetable oil
100 ml/3½ fl oz/scant ½ cup cider or
   sherry vinegar

1 Place the chicken in a pan with enough stock to cover. Bring to the boil, then reduce the heat and simmer for 5 minutes. Remove from the heat and allow the chicken to cool in the stock; the chicken will continue to cook as it cools in the hot stock.

2 Meanwhile, roast the garlic cloves in an ungreased heavy-based non-stick frying pan (skillet) until they are lightly browned on all sides and tender

inside. Remove from the heat. When cool enough to handle, squeeze the flesh from the skins and place in a bowl.

3 Grind the garlic with the pepper, cloves, oregano, salt, lime juice and three-quarters of the cumin seeds. Mix with the flour.

4 When the chicken is cool, remove from the stock and pat dry. Reserve the stock. Rub the

chicken with about two-thirds of the garlic-spice paste and stand at room temperature for at least 30 minutes or up to overnight in the refrigerator.

5 Fry the onions and chillies in a tiny bit of the oil until golden brown and softened. Pour in the vinegar and remaining cumin seeds, cook for a few minutes, then add the reserved stock and remaining spice paste. Boil, stirring, for about 10 minutes until reduced in volume.

6 Dredge the chicken in flour. Heat the remaining oil in a heavy-based frying pan (skillet). Fry the chicken until lightly browned, then remove from the pan and serve immediately, each portion topped with the onion and vinegar sauce.

Tequila-marinated Crisp Chicken Wings

The tequila tenderises these tasty chicken wings and gives them a delicious flavour. Serve as part of a barbecue, accompanied by corn tortillas, refried beans, salsa and lots of chilled lager.

Serves 4

INGREDIENTS

900 g/2 lb chicken wings
11 garlic cloves, finely chopped
juice of 2 limes
juice of 1 orange
2 tbsp tequila

1 tbsp mild chilli powder
2 tsp Chipotle Salsa (see page 98) or 2
  dried chipotle chillies, reconstituted
  (see page 100) and puréed
2 tbsp vegetable oil

1 tsp sugar
¼ tsp ground allspice
pinch of ground cinnamon
pinch of ground cumin
pinch of dried oregano

1 Cut the chicken wings into two pieces at the joint.

2 Place the chicken wing in a non-metallic dish and add the remaining ingredients. Toss well to coat, then leave to marinate for at least 3 hours or overnight in the refrigerator.

3 Cook over the hot coals of a barbecue (grill) for about 15–20 minutes or until the wings

are crisply browned, turning occasionally. To test whether the chicken is cooked, pierce a thick part with a skewer – the juices should run clear. Serve at once.

COOK'S TIP

Made from the agave plant, tequila is Mexico's famous alcoholic drink.

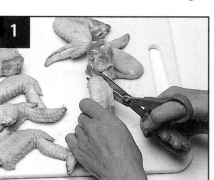

Citrus-marinated Chicken

This is a great dish for a summer meal. The marinade gives the chicken an appetizing flavour and helps keeps it succulent and moist during cooking.

Serves 4

INGREDIENTS

1 chicken, cut into 4 pieces
1 tbsp mild chilli powder
1 tbsp paprika
2 tsp ground cumin
juice and rind of 1 orange
juice of 3 limes
pinch of sugar
8–10 garlic cloves, finely chopped

1 bunch fresh coriander (cilantro), coarsely chopped
2–3 tbsp extra-virgin olive oil
50 ml/2 fl oz/¼ cup beer, tequila, or pineapple juice (optional)
salt and pepper

TO SERVE:
lime wedges
tomato, (bell) pepper and spring onion (scallion) salad
fresh coriander (cilantro) sprigs

1 Place the chicken in a non-metallic dish. To make the marinade, mix the remaining ingredients together in a bowl, seasoning with salt and pepper.

2 Pour the marinade over the chicken, turn to coat well, then leave to marinate for at least an hour at room temperature. If possible leave for 24 hours in the refrigerator to marinate.

3 Remove the chicken from the marinade and pat dry with paper towels.

4 Put the chicken on a grill (broiler) pan and place under a preheated grill (broiler) for 20–25 minutes, turning once, until the chicken is cooked through. Alternatively cook in a ridged pan. Brush with the marinade occasionally. To test whether it is cooked, pierce a thick part

with a skewer – the juices should run clear.

5 Garnish with coriander (cilantro) and serve with lime wedges and a refreshing side salad.

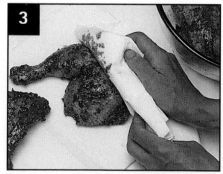

Poussins in Green Marinade

*Flavoured with a green herb marinade, these elegant poussins
are packed with lively Mexican flavours.*

Serves 4

INGREDIENTS

10 garlic cloves, chopped
juice of 1 lime
1 bunch fresh coriander (cilantro),
   finely chopped
½ fresh green chilli, deseeded and
   chopped

1 tsp ground cumin
4 poussins
350 g/12 oz/1½ cups crème fraîche
1 red (bell) pepper, roasted, peeled,
   deseeded and diced

¼–1 tsp marinade from chipotle
   canned in adobo, or chipotle salsa
3–5 spring onions (scallions), thinly
   sliced
handful of toasted pumpkin seeds
salt and pepper

1 Combine about 9 garlic
cloves with the lime juice,
about three-quarters of the fresh
coriander (cilantro), the green
chilli and half the cumin in a
bowl. Press the mixture on to the
poussins and leave to marinate for
at least 3 hours in the refrigerator
or preferably overnight.

2 Place the poussins in a roasting
tin (pan) and cook in a
preheated oven at 200°C/400°F/
Gas Mark 5 for 15 minutes.
Remove one from the oven at

this point, to check whether it is
cooked – pierce the thigh with a
knife and if the juices run clear,
the poussin is cooked. If necessary,
return to the oven and continue to
roast until cooked through.

3 Meanwhile, mix the crème
fraîche with the (bell) pepper,
chipotle marinade and remaining
garlic and cumin. Season.

4 Serve each poussin with a
spoonful of the pepper sauce
and a sprinkling of the remaining

coriander, the spring onions
(scallions) and pumpkin seeds.
Serve right away.

VARIATION

*For barbecued (grilled) lamb,
skewer lamb chunks, such as
shoulder or leg, on to metal or
soaked bamboo skewers. Marinate
in the green herbed marinade as in
Step 1, then cook over the hot coals
of a barbecue (grill) until the lamb
is cooked to your liking.*

Chicken with Purslane & Chilli

*Purslane is terribly fashionable, due to its unique flavour and healthy dose of omega-3 fatty acids.
It is a weed, and beloved by the Mexicans, who stew it as well as eat it raw.*

Serves 4

INGREDIENTS

juice of 1 lime
6 garlic cloves, finely chopped
¼ tsp dried oregano
¼ tsp dried marjoram
¼ tsp dried thyme
½ tsp ground cumin
1 chicken, cut into 4 pieces

about 10 large dried mild chillies,
 such as pasilla, toasted
450 ml/16 fl oz/2 cups boiling water
450 ml/16 fl oz/2 cups chicken stock
3 tbsp extra-virgin olive oil
700 g/1 lb 9 oz tomatoes, charred
 under the grill (broiler), skinned
 and deseeded

handful of corn tortilla chips, crushed
several large handfuls of purslane, cut
 into bite-sized lengths
½ lime
salt and pepper
lime wedges, to serve

1 Combine the lime juice, half the garlic, the oregano, marjoram, thyme, cumin and salt to taste. Rub the mixture over the chicken and leave to marinate for at least an hour, or overnight in the refrigerator.

2 Place the chillies in a pan and pour the boiling water over them. Cover and leave for 30 minutes until softened. Remove the stems and seeds. Purée the chillies in a food processor or blender, adding just enough of the stock to make a smooth paste. Add the rest of the stock and mix well.

3 Heat a tablespoon of oil in a heavy-based frying pan (skillet). Add the chilli purée with the tomatoes and remaining garlic. Cook over a medium heat, stirring, until it has thickened and reduced by about half. Set aside.

4 Remove the chicken from the marinade, reserving any marinade juices. Brown the chicken in the remaining oil, then place in flameproof casserole. Add any reserved marinade juices and the reduced chilli sauce. Cover and simmer over a low heat for about 30 minutes until the chicken is tender.

5 Stir the crushed tortillas into the sauce and cook for a few minutes. Return to the casserole and add the purslane. Season with salt, pepper and a squeeze of lime. Heat and serve with lime wedges.

Duck with Mole Sauce & Pineapple

A wonderful combination of sweet and spicy flavours, this dish is bursting with Mexican flavours.
Serve with a mixture of long-grain and wild rice for a sophisticated touch.

Serves 4

INGREDIENTS

1 duck, cut into 4 pieces
juice of 2 limes
120 ml/ 4 fl oz/½ cup pineapple juice
5–8 garlic cloves, sliced or chopped

a few shakes of mild red chilli powder,
  such as ancho
2 tbsp sugar
salt

½ pineapple, peeled and cut into slices
450 ml/16 fl oz/2 cups mole sauce
  (see page 90)
salt
fresh chilli strips, to garnish

1 Combine the duck with the lime juice, pineapple juice, garlic, chilli powder, salt and half the sugar. Leave to marinate for at least 2 hours, preferably overnight in the refrigerator.

2 Remove the duck from the marinade and pat dry with paper towels. Arrange the dark meat in a roasting tin (pan) and roast in a preheated oven at 160°C/325°F/Gas Mark 3 for about 20 minutes. Pour off the fat as it renders from the duck.

3 Add the breast pieces and continue to roast slowly for about 20 more minutes. Pour off the fat. Increase the temperature to 200–220°C/400–425°F/Gas Mark 6–7 for 5–10 minutes or until crisp and brown the duck.

4 Warm the mole sauce with enough water to prevent it from sticking and burning. Set aside and keep warm.

5 Sprinkle the pineapple with the remaining sugar and grill (broil) on both sides until the pineapple is lightly browned.

6 Serve the duck portions accompanied by the pineapple slices and topped with the mole sauce. Garnish with chilli and serve.

Turkey with Mole

In Mexican groceries you can buy a jar of mole paste – useful for when you don't have a stash of leftover mole in your refrigerator or freezer.

Serves 4

INGREDIENTS

4 turkey portions, cut into 4 pieces
about 450 ml/16 fl oz/2 cups
  chicken stock
about 225 ml/8 fl oz/ 1 cup water
1 onion, chopped
1 whole garlic bulb, divided
  into cloves and peeled
1 celery stick, chopped
1 bay leaf

1 bunch coriander (cilantro),
  finely chopped
500 ml/18 fl oz/2¼ cups mole sauce
  (see page 90) or use
  ready-made mole, thinned as
  instructed on the container

TO GARNISH:
4–5 tbsp sesame seeds
4–5 tbsp chopped fresh coriander
  (cilantro)

1 Arrange the turkey in a large flameproof casserole. Pour the stock and water around the turkey, then add the onion, garlic, celery, bay leaf and half the coriander (cilantro).

2 Cover and bake in a preheated oven at 190°C/ 375°F/Gas Mark 5 for about 1–½ hours; the turkey should be very tender. Add extra liquid if needed.

3 Warm the mole in a pan with enough stock to make it the consistency of thin cream.

4 To toast the sesame seeds for the garnish, put the seeds in an ungreased frying pan (skillet) and fry, shaking the pan, until lightly golden.

5 Arrange the turkey pieces on a serving plate and spoon the warmed mole over the top. Sprinkle with the toasted sesame seeds and chopped fresh coriander (cilantro) and serve.

Desserts & Beverages

Mexico is a land that swelters in the heat of the sun, and living there one needs constant refreshment and rehydration. The cuisine offers a wealth of drinks to slake this thirst, to refresh, to replenish: drinks based on juices or fruits mixed with milk. For a drink with a bit more punch, try tequila-based Margarita, and on the soothing side, relax with a traditional Mexican hot chocolate.

For dessert, fresh fruit, the amazing fragrant and sweet fresh fruit of Mexico, is often all you'll want, especially after the hearty and satisfying fare of this land. If you yearn for something rich however, try Churros, cinnamon-scented doughnut-like fritters, or little meringues named after the sigh of a nun.

Aztec Oranges

*Simplicity itself, this refreshing orange dessert is hard to beat and is
the perfect follow up to a hearty, spiced main course dish.*

Serves 4–6

INGREDIENTS

6 oranges
1 lime
2 tbsp tequila

2 tbsp orange-flavoured liqueur
dark soft brown sugar, to taste

fine lime rind strips, to decorate
(see Cook's Tip)

1 Using a sharp knife, cut a
slice off the top and bottom
of the oranges, then remove the
peel and pith, cutting downwards
and taking care to retain the shape
of the oranges.

2 Holding the oranges on their
side, cut them horizontally into
slices.

3 Place the oranges in a bowl.
Cut the lime in half and
squeeze over the oranges. Sprinkle
with the tequila and liqueur, then
sprinkle over sugar to taste.

4 Chill until ready to serve,
then transfer to a serving dish
and garnish with lime strips.

COOK'S TIP

*To make the decoration, finely pare
the rind from a lime using a
vegetable peeler, then cut into thin
strips. Add to boiling water and
blanch for 2 minutes. Drain in a
sieve (strainer) and rinse under cold
running water. Drain again and
pat dry with paper towels. Use this
method for orange and lemon
decorative strips as well.*

Pineapple Compote with Tequila & Mint

This light, chilled dessert is a refreshing way to finish a Mexican spread.
For a more elaborate dish, accompany the pineapple with a scoop of good-quality pineapple sorbet.

Serves 4–6

INGREDIENTS
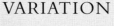

1 ripe pineapple
sugar, to taste
juice of 1 lemon

2–3 tbsp tequila or a few drops of
vanilla essence (extract)

several sprigs of fresh mint, leaves
removed and cut into thin strips
fresh mint sprig, to decorate

1 Using a sharp knife, cut off the top and bottom of the pineapple. Place upright on a board, then slice off the skin, cutting downwards. Cut in half, remove the core if wished, then cut the flesh into slices. Cut into the fruit chunks.

2 Put the pineapple in a bowl and sprinkle with the sugar, lemon juice, tequila or vanilla essence (extract).

3 Toss the pineapple to coat well, then chill until ready to serve.

4 To serve, arrange on a serving plate and sprinkle with the mint strips. Decorate the dish with a mint sprig.

COOK'S TIP

Make sure you slice off the 'eyes' when removing the skin from the pineapple.

VARIATION

Substitute 3 peeled sliced mangoes for the pineapple. To prepare mango, slice of a large piece of flesh on either side of the stone, peel and cut into chunks. Slice off the remaining flesh attached to the stone.

Oranges & Strawberries with Lime

Ideal as a summery dessert, this dish can also be served as a fresh fruit dish with brunch.
The oranges enhance the delicate flavour of the berries.

Serves 4

INGREDIENTS

3 sweet oranges 225 g/8 oz strawberries	grated rind and juice of 1 lime 1–2 tbsp caster (superfine) sugar	fresh mint sprig, to decorate

1 Using a sharp knife, cut a slice off the top and bottom of the oranges, then remove the peel and pith, cutting downwards and taking care to retain the shape of the oranges.

2 Using a small sharp knife, cut down between the membranes of the oranges to remove the segments. Discard the membranes.

3 Hull the strawberries, pulling the leaves off with a pinching action. Cut into slices, along the length of the strawberries.

4 Put the oranges and strawberries in a bowl, then sprinkle with the lime rind, lime juice and sugar. Chill until ready to serve.

5 To serve, transfer to a serving bowl and decorate the dish with a mint sprig.

VARIATION

Replace the oranges with mangoes, and the strawberries with blackberries, for a dramatically coloured dessert.

COOK'S TIP

An optional hit of orange-flavoured liqueur is delicious on this – reduce or omit the sugar.

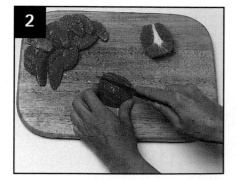

Icy Fruit Blizzard

Keep a store of prepared fruit in the freezer, then whirl it up into this refreshing dessert, which is as light and healthy as it is satisfying. You can vary the fruit as you like.

Serves 4

INGREDIENTS

1 pineapple
1 large piece deseeded watermelon, peeled and cut into small pieces

225 g/8 oz strawberries or other berries, hulled and whole or sliced
1 mango, peach or nectarine, peeled and sliced

1 banana, peeled and sliced
orange juice
caster (superfine) sugar, to taste

1 Cover 2 non-stick baking (cookie) sheets or ordinary baking (cookie) sheets with a sheet of cling film (plastic wrap). Arrange the fruit on top and freeze for at least 2 hours or until firm and icy.

2 Place one type of fruit in a food processor and process until it is all broken up into small pieces.

3 Add a little orange juice and sugar, to taste, and continue to process until it forms a granular mixture. Repeat with the

remaining fruit. Arrange in chilled bowls and serve immediately.

COOK'S TIP

The fruit can be processed all together, if preferred, or use just one type of fruit – match the juice to the fruit.

VARIATION

For an icy fruit yogurt shake, omit the pineapple and watermelon and process the remaining fruit together, replacing the juice with a half and half mix of milk and fruit yogurt.

Bunuelo Stars

*Cutting the flour tortillas into star shapes makes a whimsical treat,
and the points of the stars get deliciously crisp.*

Serves 4

INGREDIENTS

4 flour tortillas
3 tbsp ground cinnamon

6–8 tbsp caster (superfine) sugar
vegetable oil, for frying

chocolate ice cream, to serve
fine orange rind strips, to decorate

1 Using a sharp knife or kitchen scissors cut each tortilla into star shapes.

2 Mix the cinnamon and sugar together and set aside.

3 Heat the oil in a shallow wide frying pan (skillet) until it is hot enough to brown a cube of bread in 30 seconds. Working one at a time, fry the star-shaped tortillas until one side is golden, then turn and cook until golden on the other side. Remove from the hot oil with a slotted spoon and drain on paper towels.

4 Sprinkle generously with the cinnamon and sugar mixture. Serve with chocolate ice cream, sprinkled with orange rind strips.

VARIATION

Drench the bunuelos in a simple syrup, flavoured with a little cinnamon or aniseed.

COOK'S TIP

These star-shaped bunuelos make an attractive decoration for an ice cream sundae with Mexican flavours, caramel, cinnamon, coffee, chocolate.

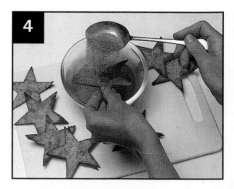

Empanadas of Banana & Chocolate

Using filo pastry makes these empanadas light and crisp on the outside, while the filling of diced banana and pieces of chocolate melt into a scrumptious hot banana-chocolate goo.

Serves 4–6

INGREDIENTS

about 8 sheets of filo pastry, cut into half lengthways
melted butter or vegetable oil, for brushing
2 ripe sweet bananas

1–2 tsp sugar
juice of ¼ lemon
175–200 g/6–7 oz dark chocolate, broken into small pieces

icing (confectioners') sugar, for dusting
ground cinnamon, for dusting

1 Working one at a time, lay a long rectangular sheet of filo out in front of you and brush it with butter or oil.

2 Peel and dice and bananas and place in a bowl. Add the sugar and lemon juice and stir well to combine. Stir in the chocolate.

3 Place a couple of teaspoons of the banana and chocolate mixture in one corner of the pastry, then fold over into a triangle shape to enclose the filling. Continue to fold in a triangular shape, until the filo is completely wrapped around the filling.

4 Dust the parcels with icing (confectioners') sugar and cinnamon. Place on a baking (cookie) sheet and continue the process with the remaining filo and filling.

5 Bake in a preheated oven at 190°C/375°F/Gas Mark 5 for about 15 minutes or until the little pastries are golden. Remove from the oven and serve hot – warn people that the filling is very hot.

COOK'S TIP
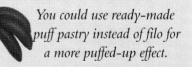
You could use ready-made puff pastry instead of filo for a more puffed-up effect.

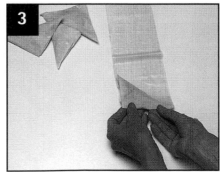

Churros

Sold on the streets of Mexico, these tempting treats can be enjoyed at any time of the day – dip them into a cup of hot chocolate for breakfast, nibble them as a mid-day snack with coffee, or serve them as part of a late-night supper.

Serves 4

INGREDIENTS

225 ml/8 fl oz/1 cup water
rind of 1 lemon
6 tbsp butter
⅛ tsp salt

125 g/4 oz/1 cup plain (all-purpose) flour
¼ tsp ground cinnamon, plus extra for dusting

½–1 tsp vanilla essence (extract)
3 eggs
vegetable oil, for frying
caster (superfine) sugar, for dusting

1 Place the water with the lemon rind in a heavy-based saucepan. Bring to the boil, add the butter and salt and cook the mixture for a few moments until the butter melts.

2 Add the flour all at once, with the cinnamon and vanilla, then remove the pan from the heat and stir rapidly until it forms the consistency of mashed potatoes.

3 Beat in the eggs, one at a time, using a wooden spoon; if you have difficulty incorporating the eggs to a smooth mixture, use a potato masher, then when it is mixed, return to a wooden spoon and mix until smooth.

4 Heat 2.5 cm/1 inch oil in a deep frying pan (skillet) until it is hot enough to brown a cube of bread in 30 seconds.

5 Place the batter in a pastry tube with a wide nozzle, then squeeze out 12 cm/5 inch lengths directly into the hot oil, making sure that the churros are about 7.5–10 cm/3–4 inches apart, as they will puff up as they cook. You may need to fry them in 2 or 3 batches.

6 Cook the churros in the hot oil for about 2 minutes on each side, until they are golden brown. Remove with a slotted spoon and drain on paper towels.

7 Dust generously with sugar and sprinkle with cinnamon to taste. Serve the dish either hot or at room temperature.

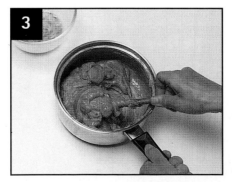

Torta de Cielo

This flat almond-flavoured sponge cake has a dense, moist texture which melts in the mouth.
The perfect accompaniment to a good strong cup of coffee for either brunch or afternoon tea.

Serves 4–6

INGREDIENTS

175 g/6 oz raw almonds, in their skins
225 g/8 oz unsalted butter, at room temperature
225 g/8 oz/1 cup plus 2 tbsp sugar
3 eggs, lightly beaten
1 tsp almond essence (extract)

1 tsp vanilla essence (extract)
9 tbsp plain (all-purpose) flour
a pinch of salt
butter, for greasing

TO SERVE:
icing (confectioners') sugar, for dusting
flaked (slivered) almonds, toasted

1 Lightly butter a 20 cm/8 inch round or square cake tin (pan) and line the tin with baking parchment.

2 Put the almonds in a food processor to form a 'mealy' mixture. Set aside.

3 Beat together the butter and sugar in a bowl until smooth and fluffy. Beat in the eggs, almonds and both the almond and vanilla essences (extracts) until well blended.

4 Stir in the flour and salt and mix briefly, until the flour is just incorporated.

5 Pour or spoon the batter into the greased tin (pan) and smooth the surface. Bake in a preheated oven at 180°C/350°F/ Gas Mark 4 for 40–50 minutes or until the cake feels spongy when gently pressed.

6 Remove from the oven, and leave to stand on a wire rack to cool. To serve, dust with icing (confectioners') sugar and decorate with toasted almonds.

Mexican Chocolate Meringues

The Mexican name for these delicate meringues is suspiros, *meaning 'sighs' – supposedly the contented sighs of the nuns who created them. They are lightly crisp on the outside, with a deliciously chewy texture centre.*

Makes about 25 meringues

INGREDIENTS

4–5 egg whites, at room temperature
a pinch of salt
¼ tsp cream of tartar
¼–½ tsp vanilla essence (extract)

175–200 g/6–7 oz/¾–1 cup caster
  (superfine) sugar
⅛–¼ tsp ground cinnamon
115 g/4 oz dark or semi-sweet
  chocolate, grated

TO SERVE:
ground cinnamon
115 g/4 oz strawberries
chocolate-flavoured cream
  (see Cook's Tip)

1 Whisk the egg whites until they are foamy, then add the salt and cream of tartar and beat until very stiff. Whisk in the vanilla, then slowly whisk in the sugar, a small amount at a time, until the meringue is shiny and stiff. This should take about 3 minutes by hand, and under a minute with an electric beater.

2 Whisk in the cinnamon and grated chocolate. Spoon mounds, about 2 tablespoonfuls,

on to an ungreased non-stick baking (cookie) sheet. Space the mounds well.

3 Place in a preheated oven at 150°C/300°F/Gas Mark 2 and cook for 2 hours until set.

4 Carefully remove from the baking (cookie) sheet. If the meringues are too moist and soft, return them to the oven to firm up and dry out more. Allow to cool completely.

5 Serve the meringues dusted with cinnamon and accompanied by strawberries and chocolate-flavoured cream.

COOK'S TIP

To make the flavoured cream, simply stir half-melted chocolate pieces into stiffly whipped cream, then chill until solid.

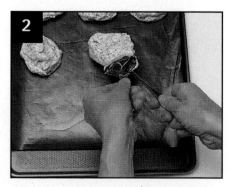

Soothing Mexican Drinks

Two milky drinks, packed with authentic Mexican flavours
– choose a cooling strawberry milkshake for a hot summer's day,
or a rich hot chocolate drink, with spicy aromas, as a winter warmer.

Serves 4

INGREDIENTS

STRAWBERRY MILKSHAKE:
450 g/1 lb strawberries
700 ml/1¼ pints/3 cups milk
225 ml/8 fl oz/1 cup strawberry
   yogurt (optional)
sugar, to taste
2 handfuls of ice cubes

MEXICAN HOT CHOCOLATE:
115–175 g/4–6 oz plain chocolate,
   broken into small pieces
½ tsp ground cinnamon
1 litre/1¾ pints/4 cups milk
dash of almond essence (extract)
dash of vanilla essence (extract)

just a few grains of salt (to bring out
   the flavour of the chocolate)
caster (superfine) sugar, to taste
2 tbsp grated chocolate
4 cinnamon sticks, to serve (optional)

1 To make the strawberry milkshake, place half the strawberries in a blender or food processor, reserving 4 for decoration. Add half milk and yogurt, if using, to the blender and process to a purée.

2 Add sugar, to taste, and ice cubes, then blend again until the ice is crushed and the drink is thick and icy. Pour into tall glasses, decorate with the

reserved strawberries and serve at once. Repeat with the rest.

3 To make the Mexican hot chocolate, gently heat the chocolate with the cinnamon and milk in a saucepan.

4 When the chocolate has melted, add the almond and vanilla essences (extracts) with the salt and sugar. Whisk together until well blended and heated through.

5 Pour into cups, sprinkle with grated chocolate and serve each cup with a cinnamon stick for stirring, if wished.

VARIATION

To vary the flavour of the milkshake, substitute raspberries, bananas or mango for the strawberries and use a yogurt of your choice.

Fruity Refreshers

These fragrant, utterly refreshing drinks are full of the tropical flavours of Mexico. They cool and revive with each sip...

Serves 4–6

INGREDIENTS

COCONUT-LIME DRINK:
450 ml/16 fl oz/2 cups coconut milk
  (unsweetened)
120 ml/4 fl oz/1 cup freshly squeezed
  lime juice
1 litre/1¾ pints/4 cups tropical fruit
  juice, such as mango, papaya, guava
  or passion fruit
sugar, to taste

crushed ice
fresh mint sprigs, to decorate

SANGRIA:
1 bottle dry full-bodied red wine
50 ml/2 fl oz orange-flavoured liqueur
50 ml/2 fl oz ¼ cup brandy
225 ml/8 fl oz/1 cup orange juice
sugar, to taste

1 orange, washed
1 lime, washed
1 peach or nectarine
½ cucumber, thinly sliced
ice cubes
bubbly mineral water, for topping up

1 To make the coconut-lime fruit drink, combine the coconut milk with the lime juice, tropical fruit juice and sugar, to taste. Add the ice and whisk until well mixed. Alternatively, place the ingredients in a food processor and process until well mixed. Serve immediately, decorated with mint leaves.

2 To make the sangria, pour the wine into a punch bowl and mix in the liqueur, brandy, orange juice and sugar, to taste. Cover and leave to infuse in the refrigerator for a few hours.

3 Just before serving, slice the orange and lime widthways. Cut the peach in half, remove the stone and slice the flesh.

4 Add the prepared fruit, cucumber and ice cubes to the punch bowl and top up with mineral water. Serve at once.

COOK'S TIP

To turn the coconut-lime drink into an alcoholic cocktail, add 2 tablespoons white rum per person. Add an extra decoration of tropical fruit pieces, threaded on to bamboo skewers.

Classic Margaritas

Margaritas are what makes a hot and sultry Mexican afternoon not only tolerable, but something to look forward to. A tropical holiday in a glass.

Serves 2

INGREDIENTS

CLASSIC MARGARITAS:
pared lime or lemon peel
salt, for dipping
3 tbsp tequila
3 tbsp orange-flavoured liqueur
3 tbsp freshly squeezed lime juice
handful of cracked ice
fine strips of lime rind, to decorate

MELON MARGARITAS:
1 small flavourful cantaloupe melon
    peeled, deseeded, and diced
several large handfuls of ice
juice of 1 lime
100 ml/3½ fl oz/scant ½ cup tequila
sugar, to taste

FROZEN PEACH MARGARITAS:
1 peach, sliced and frozen, or an equal
    amount of purchased frozen
    peaches
50 ml/2 fl oz ¼ cup tequila
50 ml/2 fl oz ¼ cup peach or orange-
    flavoured liqueur
juice of ½ lime
diced fresh peach or 1–2 tbsp orange
    juice, if needed

1 To make the classic margaritas, moisten the rim of two shallow, stemmed glasses with the lime or lemon peel, then dip the edge of the glasses in salt. Shake off the excess.

2 Put the tequila in a blender or food processor with the liqueur, lime juice and cracked ice. Process to blend well.

3 Pour the drink into the prepared glasses, taking care not to disturb the salt-coated rim. If preferred, strain the drink before pouring into the glass. Decorate with lime rind and serve.

4 To make the melon margaritas, put the melon in a food processor and process to form a purée. Add the ice, lime juice,

tequila and sugar to taste and process until smooth. Pour into chilled shallow glasses.

5 To make the frozen peach margaritas, blend the frozen fruit, tequila, liqueur and lime juice in a food processor until a thick purée. If too thick, add diced peach or orange juice to thin. Pour into chilled glasses and serve.

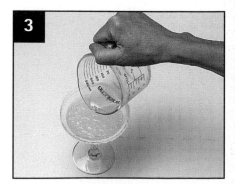

Index